The
Tenniel
Illustrations
to the
"Alice"
Books

The
Tenniel
Illustrations
to the
"Alice"
Books

By Michael Hancher

.. ——————— ..

Ohio State University Press

An earlier version of chapter 7, under the title
"John Tenniel, Horace Mayhew, and the White Knight,"
appeared in *Jabberwocky* 8 (1979): 98–107.
Reprinted by permission.

An earlier version of chapter 12, under the title
"The Placement of Tenniel's *Alice* Illustrations,"
appeared in the *Harvard Library Bulletin* 30
(1982): 237–52. Reprinted by permission.

Library of Congress Cataloging in Publication Data

Hancher, Michael, 1941–
    The Tenniel illustrations to the Alice books.
    Bibliography: p.
    Includes index.
    1. Tenniel, John, Sir, 1820–1914. A. Carroll, Lewis, 1832–1898.
Alice's adventures in Wonderland—Illustrations. 3. Carroll, Lewis,
1832–1898. Through the Looking-glass—Illustrations. I. Title.
NC978.5.T46H3   1985   741.64′2′0924   84–11842
CLOTH: ISBN 0-8142-0374-4
PAPER: ISBN 0-8142-0408-2

For my mother and in memory of my father

Contents

Illustrations

Acknowledgments

Many people have given help and encouragement to the writing of this book. I especially want to thank the following: Chester L. Anderson; Mary Ann Bonney (*Punch*); Honor Dexter; Joan Digby; Margery Durham; Félix Alfaro Fournier; John GilMartin (City of Birmingham Museums and Art Gallery); Donald J. Gray; Edward Guiliano; Elizabeth L. Hirsch; Gordon Hirsch; Park Honan; Kenneth Keller; Janis Lull; William Madden; J. Lawrence Mitchell; Angelina Morhange (The National Gallery, London); Frankie Morris; Alan F. Nagel; Stephen Prickett; Phyllis M. Rogers (Palace of Westminster, London); John B. Smith, III; Phoebe Stanton; and Michael Steig.

My wife Linda first pointed out to me the resemblance of young John Bull to Tweedledum and Tweedledee, and so confirmed my curiosity about the Tenniel illustrations. Matthew, our son, has grown almost to Alice's age in the time it has taken to write this book. It is for them both, as well as for my parents—who, along with much else, gave me my first set of the *Alice* books when I was about Matthew's age.

Cathy Aunan patiently repaired and maintained the text after it was read into a word processor by a troublesome optical scanner. Among the staff members of the University of Minnesota Libraries, Robert Jevne, Jennifer Lewis, Erika Linke, Dennis Skrade, and Herbert Scherer have been especially helpful.

I owe a special debt to Elizabeth Martin, who edited this book with great skill and forbearance.

Versions of chapters 1, 7, and 12 have appeared previously in *Lewis Carroll: A Celebration* (New York: Clarkson L. Potter, 1982); *Jabberwocky: The Journal of the Lewis Carroll Society* 8 (1979); and the *Harvard Library Bulletin* 30 (1982). Thanks are due to the editors (Edward Guiliano, Selwyn H. Goodacre, and Kenneth E. Carpenter) for their initial support and for their kind permission to reprint.

Much of the work on this book was made possible by a sabbatical leave from the University of Minnesota and a summer research grant from the Graduate School. Some of the research for chapter 12 was funded by a McMillan Travel Grant from the College of Liberal Arts. The cost of preparing many of the illustrations was underwritten by a grant from the Graduate School.

Figure 1.41 is reproduced by permission of the Royal Academy. Figures 6.3, 6.16, 6.17, and 6.22 are reproduced by courtesy of Félix Alfaro Fournier. Figures 11.5, 12.1, 12.2, 12.4, 12.7, 12.8, 12.9, and 12.11 are reproduced by permission of the Houghton Library, Harvard University. Figures 12.3, 12.5, 12.6, 12.14, 12.15, and 12.16 are reproduced by permission of the Kerlan Collection, Children's Literature Research Collections, University of Minnesota Libraries. Other acknowledgments are printed next to individual illustrations.

Introduction

The *Times*, the chief newspaper of Victorian England, first reported the existence of *Alice's Adventures in Wonderland* toward the end of an unsigned omnibus review that appeared the day after Christmas 1865. Nineteen "Christmas books" were discussed; and in keeping with the current gift-book fashion most of them featured woodcut illustrations. Seven "children's books" were relegated to the last paragraph of the review, where the reviewer discussed *Alice* immediately after a now forgotten volume of fantastic tales by James Greenwood, *The Hatchet Throwers*, which had been illustrated by Ernest Griset.[1] Griset's illustrations were "clever and funny."

> His drawing of animals is remarkable, and amid all the freedom of extravagance he manages to adhere to truth. His truthfulness, however, in the delineation of animal forms reminds us of Mr. Tenniel, who has illustrated a little work—*Alice's Adventures in Wonderland*, with extraordinary grace. Look at the first chapter of this volume, and note the rabbit at the head of it. His umbrella is tucked under his arm and he is taking the watch out of his pocket to see what o'clock it is. The neatness of touch with which he is set living before us may be seen in a dozen other vignettes throughout the volume, *the letterpress of which is by Mr. Lewis Carroll, and may best be described as an excellent piece of nonsense.*[2]

The italics are mine, not the reviewer's: note the minor credit that Carroll received. For the *Times* reviewer, as for other contemporary readers of *Alice's Adventures*, it was not Carroll's text but the set of illustrations by John Tenniel that made the book worth noticing. Three days earlier the *Pall Mall Gazette* had praised the story as well as the illustrations, but it emphasized the illustrator's name, not the author's. Later the children's journal *Aunt Judy's Magazine* would begin its review of the book with a concise and telling statement of priorities: "Forty-two illustrations by Tenniel! Why there needs nothing else to sell this book, one would think."[3]

The Reverend C. L. Dodgson probably had some such thought in mind himself when he sought out the professional artist John Tenniel to illustrate his amateur children's story. At that time "Lewis Carroll," the pseudonymous author of some fugitive light verse, was virtually unknown; and he was not much better known in proper style as "Charles Lutwidge Dodgson, M.A.," the author of two insignificant mathematical works. But Tenniel was one of the most popular artists in England. His political cartoons attracted general comment as they appeared each week in *Punch*, then the establishment humor magazine; and his drawings had decorated—and helped to sell—more than a dozen books in the previous decade. Only three years before, his sixty-nine exotic illustrations for Thomas Moore's Oriental romance *Lalla Rookh* (1861) had been described by the *Times* as "the greatest illustrative achievement of any single hand."[4] No wonder that the *Times* noticed *Alice's Adventures* mainly on account of its Tenniel illustrations.

In the last century, Carroll's fame as the author of the two *Alice* books has eclipsed that of his artist-collaborator. For a mix of reasons, Lewis Carroll, like Alice herself, has become a creature of popular legend. And yet Tenniel's own contribution to the books is probably as well known as Carroll's—perhaps more widely known, for there must be thousands of persons (children and adults alike) who are familiar with reproductions of some of the drawings, despite never having actually read the text. In a ghostly way, Tenniel retains something of his original precedence over Carroll.

But although Carroll's fame has prompted hundreds of critical studies of his art and life, Tenniel's fame has hardly been examined. Everybody knows the *Alice* pictures, but few people know much about them. In 1901 Cosmo Monkhouse produced a slight Victorian monograph on Tenniel's long career; half a century later, Frances Sarzano renewed the effort on the same minor scale; both these books dealt with the *Alice* illustrations only in passing. In 1934 Marguerite Mespoulet helpfully compared Tenniel's characters—and Carroll's—to the anthropomorphic beasts and flowers created by the popular French graphic artist J. J. Grandville. Recently the Harvard College Library published a small

volume reproducing its Tenniel sketches and drawings of
scenes from *Alice*. Aside from these efforts, there have been
no books on Tenniel, and not many significant articles.[5] The
present study would at least partially right the balance by
giving sustained attention to Tenniel's role in creating the
Alice books.

This is not the place for a full account of Tenniel's life or
career. For one thing, very little is known about his life; and
his career involved so many hundreds—indeed, thousands—
of published drawings as to greatly outweigh, if not over-
shadow, the crucial work on Carroll's two books. But the
outlines of the life and career can be simply sketched.

Tenniel was born on 28 February 1820, in London, where
he lived for the rest of his life; he was the third son of a
dancing and fencing master of Huguenot descent, John Bap-
tist Tenniel. Twenty years later, in a fencing match with his
father, Tenniel was accidentally blinded in his right eye. In
later years he would minimize the incident; and it is hard to
say how it affected his artistic career, which was already well
under way.

Largely self-taught, Tenniel may have benefited from his
childhood friendship with the sons of John Martin, the
painter. He quit his studies at the Royal Academy Schools "in
utter disgust at there being no teaching," as he recalled some
years later. Instead he joined the Clipstone Street Art Society
to practice life drawing, and frequented the British Museum
to study classical sculpture and (encouraged by Sir Frederic
Madden) books and prints of costume and medieval armor.
At age sixteen he exhibited, and sold, his first oil painting, at
the Society of British Artists. In 1837 he successfully sub-
mitted a narrative painting—a scene from Scott's *The Fortunes
of Nigel*—for exhibition at the Royal Academy, and he continued for several years to exhibit there. After submitting a
large-scale cartoon, *The Spirit of Justice*, in the national competition for fresco designs to decorate the new Houses of
Parliament, Tenniel was awarded a premium and was actually commissioned to do a fresco, although on a different
theme, Dryden's *St. Cecilia*—one of eight illustrations of
British poetry.

To learn fresco technique, Tenniel took his first (and all
but last) trip abroad, to Munich, where he studied briefly
with Peter von Cornelius, whose somewhat schematic
draftsmanship reinforced a tendency in Tenniel's own work
toward clarity and simplicity of line. In the end the British
damp so badly damaged the *St. Cecilia* that it had to be
covered up, although it did manage to outlast the other fres-
coes in the poetry group.

In later years Tenniel would gently mock his youthful
ambitions for "High Art," and certainly he prospered in the
relatively lower reaches of illustration and political caricature. As a boy he had impressed his father with a set of
drawings he had done for Bunyan's *Pilgrim's Progress*—
drawings since lost, that one would like to compare to the
drawings he did later of Alice's progress. Before long he was
publishing book illustrations: first, several for S. C. Hall's
Book of British Ballads (1842); then the set of eleven drawings
for a new edition of La Motte-Fouqué's *Undine* (1845); and
then over a hundred illustrations for the Reverend Thomas
James's new version of *Aesop's Fables* (1848), a book that confirmed Tenniel's reputation, and that led to his being offered
a position on the art staff of *Punch* two years later.

Tenniel at first contributed a few relatively small black-
and-white illustrations to that comic weekly, then more
numerous and more important cuts, until he was relied upon
to supply a full-page cartoon each week, and had become the
virtual equal on the staff of John Leech. When Leech died in
1864, Tenniel became the chief artist, a position he kept until
he retired in 1901. In the early decades, he continued to
accept commissions for book illustrations, including the well-
received *Lalla Rookh* and the *Alice* books.

Tenniel married in his early thirties, but was widowed
within two years; after that he lived a quiet domestic life, at
first with his mother-in-law and then with a sister. The Victorian *Punch* was as much a men's club as a magazine; it provided Tenniel with social amenities not unlike those that the
Reverend Dodgson enjoyed at Christ Church.

Tenniel was knighted on Prime Minister Gladstone's
recommendation in 1893, and lived almost until the age of
ninety-four. He died on 25 February 1914, only months before the Great War destroyed the gentle and genteel world
that he had known and in a way epitomized.

The following chapters focus mainly on Tenniel's *Alice*
illustrations, and on the contexts and conditions that most
affected them. The first two chapters present two general
frames of reference: Tenniel's work as a staff cartoonist for
Punch and its effect on the illustrations; and Lewis Carroll's
own illustrations for the original manuscript version of *Alice's*

Adventures. The next four chapters concentrate on details of illustration in *Alice's Adventures in Wonderland*; three further chapters focus on illustrations for *Through the Looking-Glass.* The final three chapters return to general considerations: the nature of the Carroll-Tenniel collaboration; the practical and aesthetic conditions of Victorian woodblock illustration, especially as they exemplified the always problematic relation of illustration to text; and the merits of the original layout of the *Alice* books.

Despite, or perhaps because of, the paucity of scholarship on Tenniel, over the decades much legendary tradition has accumulated around several illustrations, and I have tried to give it a thorough and critical hearing.

I think of this as a first book on the subject, not the last. In addition to the need for a biography, Tenniel's massive *Punch* career deserves a book to itself; and a *catalogue raisonné* of the many sketches, drawings, and proofs that have survived, for *Alice* as well as for other projects, would be a great asset.[6] Nonetheless, it is not too soon to begin extended study of the most famous illustrations in English literature.

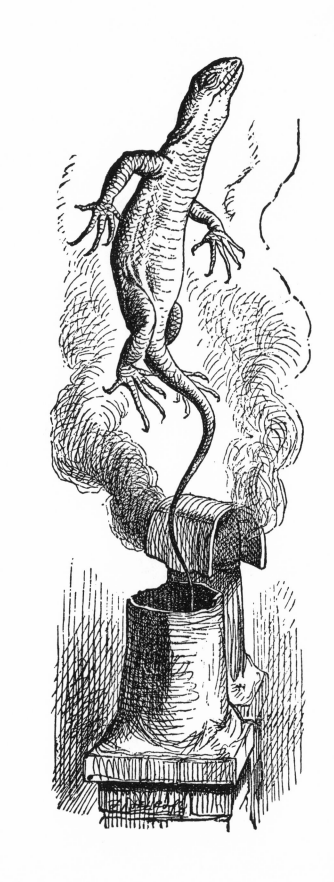

List of Abbreviations

Annotated Alice:	*The Annotated Alice*, ed. Martin Gardner. New York: Clarkson N. Potter, 1960.
Collingwood:	Stuart Dodgson Collingwood. *The Life and Letters of Lewis Carroll (Rev. C. L. Dodgson).* New York: Century, 1899.
Crutch:	*The Lewis Carroll Handbook,* ed. S. H. Williams, Falconer Madan, R. L. Green, and Denis Crutch. Folkestone, Kent: Dawson-Archon, 1979.
Diaries:	*The Diaries of Lewis Carroll,* ed. R. L. Green. 1954; rpt. Westport, Conn.: Greenwood, 1971.
Jabberwocky:	*Jabberwocky: The Journal of the Lewis Carroll Society.*
Letters:	*The Letters of Lewis Carroll,* 2 vols., ed. Morton N. Cohen. New York: Oxford University Press, 1979.
Lennon:	Florence Becker Lennon. *Victoria through the Looking-Glass: The Life of Lewis Carroll.* New York: Simon & Schuster, 1945.
Monkhouse:	Cosmo Monkhouse. *The Life and Work of Sir John Tenniel, R.I.* London: Art Journal, 1901.
OED:	*Oxford English Dictionary.*
Sarzano:	Frances Sarzano. *Sir John Tenniel.* English Masters of Black-and-White. London: Art and Technics, 1948.
Spielmann:	M. H. Spielmann: *The History of* Punch. London: Cassell, 1895
Tenniel's Alice:	*Tenniel's Alice: Drawings by Sir John Tenniel for* Alice's Adventures in Wonderland *and* Through the Looking-Glass. Cambridge: Harvard College Library, 1978.

Williams and Madan: Sidney Herbert Williams and Falconer Madan.
A Handbook of the Literature of the Rev. C. L. Dodgson
(Lewis Carroll). London: Oxford University Press, 1931.

Quotations from *Alice's Adventures in Wonderland* usually follow
the text of the first edition (London: Macmillan & Co., 1866)
as reproduced in facsimile (New York: Book League of America,
1941). Quotations from *Through the Looking-Glass* are usually
taken from the first edition (London: Macmillan & Co., 1872).
Most of the Tenniel illustrations are reproduced from the
People's Editions of the books (London: Macmillan & Co., 1887).
Most of the quotations and illustrations from *Punch* are taken
from a reprint set of the early volumes, apparently published
by the London *Times* in 1900. See R. G. G. Price, *A History
of* Punch (London: Collins, 1957), p. 346.

The
Tenniel
Illustrations
to the
"Alice"
Books

Punch *and* Alice: *Through Tenniel's Looking-Glass*

By now Tenniel's illustrations have become perfect mirror images of the world that Alice discovered down the rabbit hole and through the looking-glass. They make up the other half of the text, and readers are wise to accept no substitutes, not even those drawn by Arthur Rackham, certainly not those by Salvador Dali. This parity of word and image, unmatched in any other work of literature, fulfills the rules of symmetry set out in the second of Carroll's two *Alice* books, which is itself a reflection on the first. It also satisfies our modern and Romantic need to see in literature a hall of mirrors that gives no outlook on the world.

Nonetheless, like Alice herself, I can't help wondering if there isn't something of interest to be found on the other side of the mirror, behind (or before) the impassive surface of Tenniel's realistic fantasies. And so, like her, I will venture back and through.

The first discovery to be made on the other side is that things look much the same: Tenniel shared a world of imagery with Alice. In this respect, as in others, the *Punch* career was crucial. It was through a friend on the *Punch* staff, the dramatist and humorist Tom Taylor, that Carroll first approached Tenniel to do the *Alice* illustrations.[1] More importantly, Tenniel's growing success as the chief cartoonist of *Punch* guaranteed his work the esteem of thousands of middle-class readers.

Like us, Victorian readers would find much of Alice's strange world to be reassuringly familiar. For them, however, the familiarity would not come from having read the books and studied the pictures at age six, or from having been overexposed to the reproduction of Tenniel's images in novel contexts (such as IBM advertisements), but from having been granted frequent previews of Wonderland in images drawn for *Punch* by Tenniel and his colleagues on the staff.

Some years ago Frances Sarzano noted in passing that the *Alice* books "harvest the work of early days on *Punch*." Before

that, Marguerite Mespoulet had shown that the humanized animals of Carroll's text and of Tenniel's illustrations must have evolved from the grotesqueries drawn by Grandville for the French prototype of *Punch*, the journal *Charivari*.[2] Humanoid and fashionably dressed animals multiply in the pages of *Punch* both immediately before and throughout Tenniel's career there. What I want to draw attention to are certain *Punch* illustrations by Tenniel and others that are not so obviously in Grandville's tradition, but that reflect light also on the pages of Carroll's books.

Since image reflection is our inevitable topic, Tweedledum and Tweedledee are obvious subjects (fig. 1.1, which was drawn, like all the *Looking-Glass* illustrations, sometime between the end of 1869 and the middle of 1871). Here, on the far side of the looking-glass, each identical twin represents only the other. But on the near side, where Alice begins and ends her journey, both resemble John Bull, that embodiment of everyday England, at an age when he might be styled

Fig. 1.1. Tenniel. Alice with Tweedledum and Tweedledee. From *Through the Looking-Glass.*

Master John Bull (fig. 1.2; 27 April 1861). Under the anxious eyes of his mother, Britannia (judging from the unusual crest on the ordinary bonnet), Master Bull is accepting an anodyne of a small reduction in the income tax from his considerate dentist, William E. Gladstone, then chancellor of the exchequer. He looks almost as distressed as Tweedledum (fig. 1.3).

Fig. 1.3. Tenniel. Tweedledum. From *Through the Looking-Glass.*

Like many of the *Punch* drawings by Tenniel to be cited in this book, the Gladstone tax cartoon is unsigned; it does not bear the familiar monogram,

Tenniel signed his work occasionally from early 1851 (shortly after he joined the *Punch* staff) until early 1853, and more regularly from August 1862 on; but during the intervening decade his abundant work for *Punch* bore no signature, and much of the early work is unsigned also. Still, there is rarely any question whether a particular drawing is his; the styles in which he worked are distinctive enough.

Like the twins, Tenniel's young John Bull wears a "skeleton suit," standard for schoolboys early in the century: a high-waisted, tight-fitting jacket, usually dark, decorated in front with two or three vertical rows of buttons, with the shirt collar worn out, and ankle-length high-waisted trousers, usually light in color, buttoned over the jacket—worn with white socks and black shoes. The frilled shirt collar of figure 1.2 was out of fashion by 1830, when the twins' flat, turned-down collar replaced it. The whole outfit, common during Tenniel's boyhood, was archaic by the time he started draw-

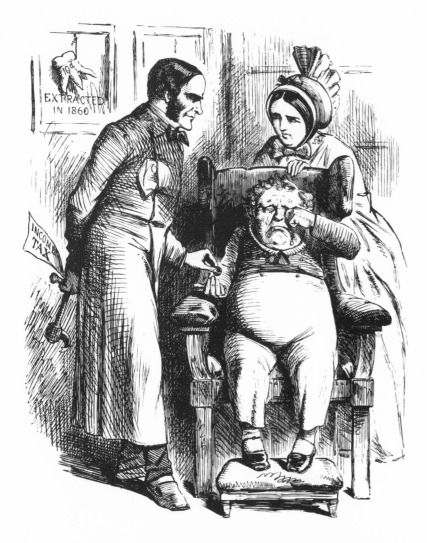

Fig. 1.2. Tenniel. "Master Bull and His Dentist." From *Punch*, 27 April 1861. The caption to the original drawing was badly faded in the impression reproduced here and became illegible in the photocopy made for this text. It reads: "MASTER BULL AND HIS DENTIST./DENTIST. 'DON'T CRY, MY LITTLE MAN! I'M NOT GOING TO DRAW ANY MORE THIS TIME, AND/THERE'S A PENNY FOR YOU!'"

Fig. 1.4. Tenniel. Young John Bull in Mr. Punch's classroom. From *Punch*, 28 June 1856.

ing *Punch* cartoons—not to mention the pictures for *Through the Looking-Glass*. If the twins, "two fat little men," are about forty years old, they are still wearing the clothes that they knew when they were children. Alice is so struck by their looking "exactly like a couple of great schoolboys"—from the past, as Tenniel drew them—that she immediately takes on the role of schoolmistress, calling out "First Boy!" and "Next Boy!," starting off their relationship on the wrong foot.[3]

A few years before the Gladstone cartoon, Tenniel had shown little John Bull dressed as a schoolboy in Mr. Punch's schoolroom of western nations, where he is being defied by a rambunctious Jonathan (the United States) for having tried to take some toy soldiers (fig. 1.4, from the preface to volume 30, dated 28 June 1856). During the previous months the Pierce administration had sharply cooled its relations with Great Britain, partly because British agents had actively recruited soldiers for the Crimean War in the United States. (Master Bull's Tweedle-twin in the background, wearing the paper hat labeled "BOMBA," is Ferdinand II, King of the Two Sicilies, popularly known as "King Bomba," who had been censured by England and France for committing atrocities against his own subjects. Among other things he had ordered the bombardment of major cities in Sicily—hence the nickname.)

As late as 1882, ten years after *Looking-Glass* was published, Tenniel's young John Bull still looks like a prototype for

THE LATEST ARRIVAL.

Fig. 1.5. Tenniel. "The Latest Arrival." From *Punch*, 7 January 1882.

Tweedledee and Tweedledum (see fig. 1.5, the New Year's cartoon published 7 January 1882). Tenniel's political cartoons were conservative artistically as well as politically; he did not change his stock of imagery much during his long career. The first historian of *Punch*, M. H. Spielmann, noticed that the way Tenniel drew a locomotive hardly changed, even as actual locomotives evolved into more and more modern forms. Tenniel's persistent image of the fat, skeleton-suited schoolboy is another example. The new, realistic style of black-and-white illustration that emerged in the sixties, inspired in part by the work of J. E. Millais, put great stock in the close observation of concrete detail, usually

contemporary, and the conscientious use of models; but after his apprenticeship Tenniel would have nothing to do with models, and relied instead on what he remembered of what he had seen.[4] The result was that his drawings, including his illustrations for the *Alice* books, tended to conserve and renew the imagery of the recent and not-so-recent past. In particular, Tenniel renewed in the *Alice* books imagery that was already established in *Punch*.

When relations between Carroll's Tweedledum and Tweedledee deteriorate to the point where the two have to be armed for battle, Tenniel pictures the scene (fig. 1.6) in a way that not only responds to Carroll's description but also

Fig. 1.6. Tenniel. Tweedledum and Tweedledee armed for combat. From *Through the Looking-Glass.*

recalls the supposed mock-heroics of the Chartist movement as they were interpreted for *Punch* by John Leech (fig. 1.7; July-December 1848, p. 101).[5] The Chartist included in one suit of armor the dish-cover breastplate of Tweedledum and the coal-scuttle helmet of Tweedledee. Tweedledum's own saucepan helmet closely resembles the new hat for London bobbies that *Punch* proposed in 1865 (fig. 1.8; 25 February 1865, by an anonymous artist). A few years before that, Tenniel had illustrated the transformation of utensils into helmets, as part of a parody of nineteenth-century researches into the history of costume (fig. 1.9; 9 June 1860—a specific parody of fig. 1.10).[6]

The mild hostility between England and the United States that marked the mid fifties had worsened a good deal by the early years of the Civil War. When the U.S.S. *Jacinto* stopped

A PHYSICAL FORCE CHARTIST ARMING FOR THE FIGHT.

Fig. 1.7. John Leech. "A Physical Force Chartist Arming for the Fight." From *Punch*, July–December 1848.

Fig. 1.8. Saucepan-hat for London bobby. From *Punch*, 25 February 1865.

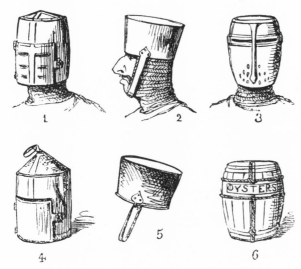

1, 2, 3. HELMETS. TEMP. RICHARD THE FIRST AND JOHN.
4, 5, 6. THE SAME IN THEIR PRIMITIVE SHAPE.
FROM MR. PUNCH'S ARCHÆOLOGICAL MUSEUM.

Fig. 1.9. Tenniel. Helmets and utensils; a parody of figure 1.10. From *Punch*, 9 June 1860.

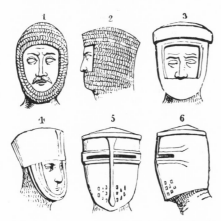

Fig. 1.10. F. W. Fairholt. Medieval helmets. From *Costume in England* (1846; 2d ed., 1860).

the British steamer *Trent* and seized two Confederate envoys, the British responded with threats of war that in the end forced the Lincoln administration to release the two (the so-called "*Trent* affair"). Tenniel depicted the outcome for *Punch* by showing Abraham Lincoln as a raccoon treed by John Bull—who is now his adult self, and an honorary "Colonel" as well (fig. 1.11; 11 January 1862).[7] The vertical relation of the two figures in this cartoon is the same as in the famous illustration, drawn some three years later, of Alice

"UP A TREE."
Colonel Bull and the Yankee 'Coon.
'Coon. "AIR YOU IN ARNEST, COLONEL?"
Colonel Bull "I AM."
'Coon. "DON'T FIRE—I'LL COME DOWN."

Fig. 1.11. Tenniel. " 'Up a Tree': Colonel Bull and the Yankee 'Coon." From *Punch*, 11 January 1862.

and the Cheshire Cat (fig. 1.12); and the perspective is precisely reversed, as is the orientation of the tree branch on which each animal is perched.

Tenniel may have based the design of the Lincoln cartoon on Gillray's rendering of Francis Russell, the duke of Bedford, as a hapless squirrel falling from an aristocratic height into entanglement with the predatory snake Charles James Fox (fig. 1.13). The caricature, originally published in 1795, would have been readily available to Tenniel in a collection of Gillray's work published in 1851.[8]

Fig. 1.12. Tenniel. Alice and the Cheshire Cat. From *Alice's Adventures in Wonderland*.

Fig. 1.13. James Gillray. "The Republican Rattle-Snake fascinating the Bedford Squirrel." Engraving. From *The Works of James Gillray* (1851; rpt. 1968).

One of the simpler reflections in the *Alice* books of Tenniel's work for *Punch* is the drawing of Humpty Dumpty addressing the messenger (fig. 1.14). Especially as regards the character on the left, it mirrors the contemporary illustration of a giant Grandvillian gooseberry addressing an even more Grandvillian frog (fig. 1.15; 15 July 1871), who in

Fig. 1.14. Tenniel. Humpty Dumpty and the messenger. From *Through the Looking-Glass.*

THE GIGANTIC GOOSEBERRY.

G. G. "HERE'S A PRECIOUS GO, FROGGY! I THOUGHT BIG GOOSEBERRIES AND SHOWERS O' FROGS UD HAVE A HOLIDAY THIS 'SILLY SEASON,' ANYHOW. BUT THE PRECIOUS TICHBORNE CASE HAVE BEEN ADJOURNED, AND WE'LL HAVE TO BE ON DUTY AGAIN."

Fig. 1.15. Tenniel. "The Gigantic Gooseberry." From *Punch*, 15 July 1871.

Fig. 1.16. Tenniel. The Frog-Footman and the Fish-Footman. From *Alice's Adventures in Wonderland.*

Fig. 1.17. Tenniel. Alice with the White Queen and the Red Queen. From *Through the Looking-Glass.*

turn recalls the demeanor of the Frog-Footman in *Alice's Adventures* (fig. 1.16). (The gigantic gooseberry and the background shower of frogs are allusions to stock "filler" items, reporting supposed wonders of nature, which filled the popular press during the slow summer months, when there was usually a dearth of official news, and which *Punch* never tired of ridiculing).[9]

Perhaps more subtle reflections would have caught the Victorian reader's eye more immediately. Some early readers may have noticed how Tenniel's White Queen and Red Queen (fig. 1.17) renew the association in *Punch* of Mrs. Gamp and her imaginary friend Mrs. Harris—the besotted pair from *Martin Chuzzlewit*—who served as emblems of the look-alike *Standard* and *Herald* newspapers (fig. 1.18, by Tenniel's mentor John Leech; 9 April 1864). Note the crinoline apparatus displaying itself beneath the White Queen's dress, and beneath Mrs. Gamp's. *Punch* waged a relentless war against the vanity and vulgarity of crinolines, then the current fashion.[10] *Punch* also disdained the Pope (Pius IX), and loved to show him effeminate and helpless in crinolines (fig. 1.19, by Tenniel; 20 September 1862).[11] In general posture this Pope is every inch a White Queen (fig. 1.20, drawn nine years later).

That *Punch* thought the Papacy to be a caterpillar on the English landscape can be judged from the conjunction of two more or less irreverent images, figure 1.21, by Tenniel (January–June 1855, p. 67), and figure 1.22, by Leech (January–June 1851, p. 35): taken together, they yielded the now well-known image of the arrogant Caterpillar savoring his hookah on a toadstool (fig. 1.23).[12] The hookah was a common motif in the fantasies of the *Punch* staff, which often boasted Arabian or Oriental decor; in one instance it was accompanied by a psychedelic mushroom (fig. 1.24, by H. R. Howard; 20 October 1860).

Even as in the *Alice* books, orality in *Punch* could take more aggressive forms than placid hookah-smoking. A trope shared by both publications, very common in *Punch*, shows animated foodstuffs in danger. The well-known scene of the Walrus and the Carpenter addressing the Oysters (fig. 1.25), for example, is a recasting of Tenniel's cartoon of the English beef admonishing the German sausages under the gaze of the French wine (fig. 1.26; 9 January 1864).[13] Oysters had been personified before in a *Punch* drawing, perhaps by Tenniel (fig. 1.27; July–December 1853, p. 244). The personified beef and wine look forward, also, to the disturbing dinner-

THE IDLE GOSSIPS.

MRS. GAMP (TO MRS. HARRIS, SNEERING AT THE AGE OF DEAR OLD PAM). "WHAT I SAY IS—HE'S TOO OLD TO BE A CONDUCTOR—WE WANTS SMART YOUNG CHAPS LIKE YOUNG DARBY AND YOUNG DIZZY!" [*See page* 146.

Fig. 1.18. John Leech. "The Idle Gossips." From *Punch*, 9 April 1864.

RELIEVING GUARD.

Mrs. Pope. "OH, MR. POLICEMAN, I HOPE YOU AIN'T A-GOIN' TO LEAVE A POOR OLD 'OMAN?"

Mr. Nap "YES M'M I AM—YOU WILL BE QUITE SAFE WITH YOUR FRIEND, VICTOR, YONDER. HE'S A CAPITAL OFFICER."

Fig. 1.19. Tenniel. "Relieving Guard." From *Punch*, 20 September 1862.

Fig. 1.20. Tenniel. The White Queen and Alice. From *Through the Looking-Glass*.

Fig. 1.21. Tenniel. Nicholas Cardinal Wiseman. From *Punch*, January–June 1855.

THE POPE IN HIS CHAIR.

With Mr. Punch's Compliments to Lady Morgan.

Fig. 1.22. John Leech. "The Pope in His Chair."
From *Punch*, January–June 1851.

Fig. 1.23. Tenniel. The Caterpillar and Alice.
From *Alice's Adventures in Wonderland*.

Fig. 1.24. H. R. Howard. Mushroom and hookah. From *Punch*,
20 October 1860.

Fig. 1.25. Tenniel. The Walrus and the Carpenter. From *Through the Looking-Glass.*

ORIGINAL SKETCH BY MR. PUNCH'S LITTLE BOY.

Fig. 1.27. Oyster shell and bonnet. From *Punch*, July–December 1853.

THE ENGLISH BEEF, THE FRENCH WINE, AND THE GERMAN SAUSAGES.

THE BEEF. "NOW, LOOK HERE, YOU 'SMALL GERMANS,' DON'T JUMP OUT OF THE FRYING-PAN INTO THE FIRE—THAT'S ALL!"

Fig. 1.26. Tenniel. "The English Beef, the French Wine, and the German Sausages." From *Punch*, 9 January 1864.

Fig. 1.28. Tenniel. Leg of mutton. From *Through the Looking-Glass.*

A CHRISTMAS VISITOR.

Fig. 1.29. Frank Bellew (?). "A Christmas Visitor." From *Punch*, 19 January 1861.

party that concludes *Looking-Glass*, especially to the personified leg of mutton (fig. 1.28), the bottles that turn into birds, and the recalcitrant pudding. When Alice tries to treat the pudding as just an ordinary pudding, and takes a slice out of it, Carroll has it talk back to her much like the pudding in a cartoon that was probably drawn by Frank Bellew, figure 1.29 (19 January 1861).[14] Tenniel pictures Alice's pudding only once, as part of the general confusion that ends the banquet (fig. 1.30); it is easy to miss in the lower left-hand corner, opposite the mutton (appropriately), upside down, a dim look of perplexity appearing on its face/body.

A prototype for all the *Punch* cartoons cited here (and others, similar) is a drawing by Leech for the 1844 *Punch* almanac (fig. 1.31, on the page for February).[15] Leech's mentor George Cruikshank had published a drawing with similar details in his *Comic Almanack* for 1841 (fig. 1.32, December).[16] No doubt this tradition of illustration was as influential on Carroll as it was on Tenniel.

When the Carpenter finally sets to work devouring the Oysters (fig. 1.33), he strikes a pose identical to that of an oyster-eating lawyer in Tenniel's cartoon "Law and Lunacy," drawn almost a decade earlier (fig. 1.34; 25 January 1862). A satire on the way that court costs were consuming the large inheritance of an heir said by his guardian to be insane, the

drawing alludes to a proverb on the injustice of the law in the matter of court costs: "A shell for him, and a shell for thee, / The oyster is the lawyer's fee."[17]

This proverb, which associates oysters with the sharp practices of lawyers, occasions a complaint by some high-minded oysters to the reform-minded lord chancellor Lord Bethell, in a doggerel fable in the manner of John Gay's *Fables* (1727), called "Reversing the Proverb" (4 June 1864). This fable, which was illustrated by Tenniel (fig. 1.35) even while he was working on the illustrations for *Alice's Adventures*, probably was noticed by Carroll at the time, and had its echo years

Fig. 1.30. Tenniel. End of the banquet. From *Through the Looking-Glass*.

THE DUKE OF CAMBRIDGE RECEIVING AN INVITATION TO A CHARITY DINNER ON HIS BIRTHDAY.

Fig. 1.31. John Leech. "The Duke of Cambridge Receiving an Invitation to a Charity Dinner on His Birthday." From *Punch*, almanack for 1844.

LAW AND LUNACY;
Or, A Glorious Oyster Season for the Lawyers.

DECEMBER   A Swallow at Christmas. (Rara avis in terris)

Fig. 1.33. Tenniel. The Walrus and the Carpenter devouring the Oysters. From *Through the Looking-Glass.*

Fig. 1.32. George Cruikshank.
"December: 'A Swallow at Christmas.'"
From *Comic Almanack for 1841* (rpt. 1912).

Fig. 1.34 (opposite).   Tenniel. "Law and Lunacy."
From *Punch*, 25 January 1862.

Fig. 1.35. Tenniel. "Reversing the Proverb."
From *Punch*, 4 June 1864.

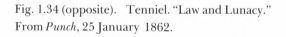

REVERSING THE PROVERB.

"The Oyster where it ought to be, | And Shell and Shell the Lawyer's Fee."

later in the pathetic colloquy of the Oysters, the Walrus, and the Carpenter. As Lord Bethell was about to enjoy a luncheon of oysters, ale, bread, and butter,

> An Oyster thus addressed my Lord,
> Not in a whistling timid key,
> But in a voice well-trained at sea.
>
> "Ho! Equity's great guard and friend!
> Attention and assistance lend."
>
> . . . .
>
> "My Lord," the Oyster said again,
> (Edging away from the Cayenne)
> "We ask relief, nor singly come,
> But in the name of Oysterdom.
> Too long, my Lord, a proverb old
> Links us with justice missed, or sold,
> Too long we've been the ribald type
> Of all who'd give the law a wipe,
> And now we hold it fitting time
> That you should quite reverse the rhyme."

After some discussion Bethell tells the Oyster that he has already accomplished the desired reforms.

> "Henceforth the rhyme that carries smart
> To my poor Oyster's oozy heart,
> Shall in another fashion run,
> And thus be passed by sire to son:
> 'The Oyster where it ought to be,
> And shell and shell the lawyer's fee.' "
>
> Again he smiled, so says the fable,
> And drew his chair up near the table,
> When all the Oysters, seen and hid,
> Cried, "Eat, and welcome." And he did.

So ends "Reversing the Proverb," on much the same note as Carroll's own fable of oysters, pepper, bread, and butter:

> "O Oysters," said the Carpenter,
> "You've had a pleasant run!
> Shall we be trotting home again?"
> But answer came there none—
> And this was scarcely odd, because
> They'd eaten every one.

The Carpenter's hat (figs. 1.25, 1.33) is, of course, the standard paper cap of the mid-Victorian workingman, which Tenniel had occasion to draw many times; for example, figure 1.36 (22 June 1861; see also July–December 1853, p. 169; 6 April 1861; 5 September 1863; and 4 August 1866). Tenniel's habit of drawing carpenters may have determined his choice of that character type when Carroll put the choice to him. (Having at first objected to the Carpenter, Tenniel

THE STRIKE.—HITTING HIM HARD.

NON-UNIONIST. "AH, BILL! I WAS AFRAID WHAT *YOUR* UNION WOULD END IN"

Fig. 1.36. Tenniel. "The Strike.—Hitting Him Hard." From *Punch*, 22 June 1861.

Fig. 1.37. Tenniel. Father William doing his headstand.
From *Alice's Adventures in Wonderland*.

Fig. 1.39. Tenniel. Father William balancing an eel on his
nose. From *Alice's Adventures in Wonderland*.

Fig. 1.38. Tenniel. Mr. Punch and his family. From *Punch*, July– December 1856.

finally preferred him to either of the two dactylic replacements that Carroll had obligingly offered, "baronet" or "butterfly.")

As well as the foreground figures in *Alice*, the backgrounds too sometimes derive from *Punch*. Two of the four Tenniel drawings that illustrate the poem "Father William" are landscapes, and both have their prototypes in the magazine. The field in which Father William does his headstand (fig. 1.37) had already served as a resort for Mr. Punch and his family (fig. 1.38, by Tenniel; July–December 1856, p. 1; note the hay rakes and pitchforks). When Father William balances an eel on the end of his nose (fig. 1.39), he does so before a background that may perplex the modern reader, but that would have been familiar to anyone who had frequented a riverbank in the middle of the nineteenth century or, failing that, who had read *Punch* or looked at certain lesser nineteenth-century landscape paintings. The structure in the right background is an eel weir or set of eel bucks, wicker baskets used to trap eels—a detail appropriate to a scene in which a man balances an eel on his nose. Leech made eel bucks the dominant elements in the design of his cartoon of Mr. Briggs, the sports enthusiast, setting out on a doomed fishing expedition (fig. 1.40; July–December 1850, p. 94). Eel weirs are pictured in *Punch* in July–December 1853, p. 142, and 23 April 1859, as well; Tenniel himself used one again as a background motif as late as 22 April 1876. William Müller did several paintings and drawings that exploit the picturesque qualities of this rustic architecture, and a painting by Frederick Richard Lee, *Morning in the Meadows* (fig. 1.41), shows this minor genre at its most pleasant.[18]

One final background, displayed in figure 1.42 (July–December 1853, title page), may suggest how nearly equivalent Punch and Alice were for Tenniel. The Romanesque doorway from which Punch distributes his largesse (bound volumes of *Punch*) is virtually the same door at which Alice demands admission to her royal prerogatives (fig. 1.43). These are not the only Romanesque doorways that Tenniel drew; he had an antiquarian fondness for the style. Still, the resemblance is striking.

And what of Alice herself? What place does she have in *Punch*'s England? She plays essentially the same role there as her usual role in the *Alice* books, that of a pacifist and noninterventionist, patient and polite, slow to return the aggressions of others. At the end of June 1864, when he had read Carroll's manuscript but probably had not yet begun drawing the illustrations for *Alice's Adventures*, Tenniel put Alice in the center of a patriotic *Punch* title page (fig. 1.44; January–June 1864). Only a few days had passed since Palmerston's cabinet had decided, in a narrow but momentous vote, not to intervene against Bismarck in the deteriorating Schleswig-Holstein affair, which had become a war between the German states and Denmark. The decision, which Parliament quickly confirmed, proved Palmerston's earlier vague threats to be empty, but the English public in general greeted it with "relief at having escaped the horrors of war." In this cartoon Tenniel fittingly images that relief in domestic terms. The English cannon stands at the ready, but only to protect the domestic scene; and the British lion is changed from a ferocious agent of war to a noble household pet, suitable to amuse boys or girls.[19]

In decorating that militant animal with the garlands of peace, Alice is much more at her ease than she is later in *Alice's Adventures*, when she confronts the officious Do-Do-Dodgson (fig. 1.45). But though her demeanor is thus subtly different in the two images, the figure and the posture are essentially the same. Of course no reader in the middle of 1864, when this *Punch* frontispiece appeared, could have recognized Alice in this her first appearance. And by the time, a year and a half later, she finally appeared as herself in *Alice's Adventures*, the old image from *Punch* would have slipped from memory. Yet, like the absent-minded White Rabbit, the Victorian reader might well suppose that he already knew who Alice was.

Alice is not the only veteran from *Punch* to appear in figure 1.45: the ape peering out from behind the Dodo shows the same face as the villainous King Bomba, who in figure 1.46 (11 October 1856) seeks the support of Russia after having been censured by England and France.[20]

Conversely, figure 1.44 is not Alice's only appearance in *Punch*. *Punch's Almanack* for 1865, published a year before *Alice's Adventures*, contains a page for July and August on which Alice figures as the astrological sign Virgo, in the form of a statue of the modest and long-suffering Joan of Arc (fig. 1.47). The facial aspect and Pre-Raphaelite hair are virtually the same as in figure 1.48, which shows Alice undergoing one of her early ordeals. A late-summer harvest scene is depicted in the tapestry hanging behind this statue, and Tenniel plays wittily with the frames of these disparate art objects by having the virtual reality of the statue impinge on the virtual reality of the tapestry. The mower closest in the fore-

Fig. 1.40. John Leech.
"Mr. Briggs Starts on His Fishing Excursion."
From *Punch*, July–December 1850.

Fig. 1.41. Frederick Richard Lee.
Morning in the Meadows. Painting.
Reproduced by permission of
the Royal Academy of Arts,
London.

Fig. 1.42. Tenniel. Mr. Punch distributing bound volumes of *Punch*. From *Punch*, July–December 1853.

Fig. 1.43. Tenniel. Queen Alice demanding admission. From *Through the Looking-Glass*.

Fig. 1.45. Tenniel. Alice and the Dodo. From *Alice's Adventures in Wonderland*.

PUNCH

VOL 46

Fig. 1.44. Tenniel. Alice figure garlanding the British lion. From *Punch*, January–June 1864.

Fig. 1.46 . Tenniel. "Bomba's Big Brother." From *Punch*, 11 October 1856.

BOMBA'S BIG BROTHER.

Emperor of Russia. "THEY SHAN'T TAKE AWAY HIS PLAYTHINGS, THAT THEY SHAN'T"

Fig. 1.47. Tenniel. "Leo" and "Virgo."
From *Punch's Almanack for 1865.*

Fig. 1.48. Tenniel. Alice outgrowing the room. From *Alice's Adventures in Wonderland.*

Fig. 1.49. Tenniel. The gardeners painting the Queen's roses. From *Alice's Adventures in Wonderland.*

Fig. 1.50. Tenniel. The Lion and the Unicorn. From *Through the Looking-Glass*.

CONSTANTINE PRY'S VISIT TO ENGLAND.

"JUST DROPPED IN—HOPE I DON'T INTRUDE—OFF AGAIN TO-MORROW."

Fig. 1.52. Tenniel. "Constantine Pry's Visit to England." From *Punch*, 13 June 1857.

Fig. 1.51. Tenniel. The British lion and the Scottish unicorn. From *Punch*, January–June 1853.

ground appears amazed to discover, behind a sheaf of wheat, this heroic image of maidenhood. The amazement may be in part the shock of recognition, for this mower and his colleagues look much like the gardeners who painted the Queen's roses red (fig. 1.49), whom Alice protected.

Opposite this Virgo stands Leo, the British lion, already seen paired with Alice in the peace cartoon (fig. 1.44). But unlike the mowers in the tapestry, this figure does not put in an appearance in *Alice's Adventures*. When he does appear in *Looking-Glass*, opposite the Unicorn (fig. 1.50), he wears a bemused look, which is called for in the text, and a pair of spectacles, which are not. ("The Lion had joined them . . . he looked very tired and sleepy, and his eyes were half shut. 'What's this!' he said, blinking lazily at Alice.") The spectacles are an old attribute, dating from 1853 at least (January–June, p. 57), some twenty years before: in figure 1.51 the English lion protests to a Scottish unicorn that he should not be displaced from the royal arms of the United Kingdom by "an obsolete quadruped calling itself the Lion of Scotland," despite a recent proposal by some Scotsmen. The squib accompanying this drawing is cast in the form of a letter from "The British Lion" to the lord responsible for the royal arms. The tone is one of formal indignation, like that of a typical letter to the *Times;* evidently this lion is at home in his study, so the pair of spectacles is quite in order. A few years later they help in reading a newspaper, no doubt the *Times* (fig. 1.52; 13 June 1857).[21]

It is unlikely that Alice, before or after her visits to Wonderland and through the looking-glass, ever paid much attention to the *Times;* for her standard for a worthwhile book, at least, called for an ample stock of "pictures" and "conversations." The *Times* during this period was long on parliamentary debates and law reports—which involve conversations of a peculiar sort—but it was very short on pictures. This lack was in large part supplied by *Punch*, which, after its salad days of radicalism, settled down to provide a comic and largely visual supplement to the somber and verbal newspaper of record—so that Tenniel gradually became the quasi-official political cartoonist of England. If indeed Alice would not have looked at the *Times*, she might well have looked at *Punch* now and again, not so much for the conversations as for the pictures, in some of which she would have recognized herself and her world, as in a looking-glass.

CHAPTER TWO

The Carroll Illustrations

The first of the many illustrators of Lewis Carroll's *Alice* books was not John Tenniel but Carroll himself. Before he had elaborated his children's story into the fully developed version that was published as *Alice's Adventures in Wonderland*, Carroll prepared a hand-lettered manuscript of an earlier version, titled *Alice's Adventures under Ground*, as a gift for Alice Liddell. It is clear from the first paragraph of this manuscript that the Alice of the story disliked books that lacked pictures: " 'What is the use of a book,' thought Alice, 'without pictures or conversations?' " By this logic Carroll's gift book had to have illustrations. Fortunately Carroll, though not a trained nor even skilled draftsman, had done such work before; as a boy he had illustrated several manuscript "magazines" that he had composed to entertain his brothers and sisters.

More than twenty years after Carroll presented his illustrated manuscript to Alice Liddell, he arranged for it to be published in facsimile, and it has been reprinted several times since.[1] In recent decades the manuscript has received much publicity as a treasured possession of the British Library.

The established view has been that Carroll's illustrations to *Alice's Adventures under Ground* were not an important influence on Tenniel's drawings for *Alice's Adventures in Wonderland*. The opinion of one of Carroll's early bibliographers, Falconer Madan, has proven influential: "In spite of some inevitable similarities, it may be doubted whether Tenniel derived any ideas directly from this book, though he may have seen it."[2] But it is very likely that Tenniel did indeed see the Carroll illustrations, and, furthermore, that they helped shape his drawings for the book.

Recently a relevant letter has been published, one that Carroll wrote to Tom Taylor, the popular dramatist who was on the staff of *Punch*. In it Carroll raised for the first time the question whether Tenniel could be persuaded to do the illustrations for *Alice's Adventures*; and he continued, "If he

should be willing to undertake them, I would send him the book to look over, not that he should at all follow my pictures, but simply to give him an idea of the sort of thing I want."[3]

Although it was apparently Carroll's intention to arrange for this commission by correspondence, he actually put the proposal to Tenniel in person, during a visit on 25 January 1864, a visit that he made armed with a letter of introduction from Taylor. At that time Carroll recorded in his diary that Tenniel "was very friendly, and seemed to think favourably of undertaking the pictures, but must see the book before deciding." On 5 April Carroll added this entry: "Heard from Tenniel that he consents to draw the pictures for *Alice's Adventures Underground*." Presumably in the interval Tenniel had seen "the book."

The book that Tenniel would have seen at that time could not have been precisely the same book that Carroll ultimately gave to Alice Liddell on 26 November, for Carroll did not finish the pictures in that manuscript until 13 September.[4]

Either the manuscript that Carroll showed Tenniel that spring was incomplete, with only some illustrations, or else it was a preliminary illustrated version, since lost. (In early 1863 Dodgson had lent to the family of George MacDonald a manuscript version of *Alice's Adventures*: it is not known whether this had any illustrations, or what its relation was to the gift manuscript.) However, Tenniel may have had an opportunity to see the completed gift manuscript when Carroll visited him in October, a month after Carroll finished it and more than a month before he gave it to Alice. During that visit Carroll and Tenniel "discussed the book and agreed on about thirty-four pictures," only eight short of the final total. Presumably Carroll had the major say in deciding which narrative moments to illustrate—if his practice in this case was like his typical practice in commissioning illustrations for his later books.[5]

Many years after the fact, Alice Liddell herself recalled

that "as a rule Tenniel used Mr. Dodgson's drawings as the basis for his own illustrations."[6] This testimony finds support in a comparison of the pictures themselves.

One basis for comparison is the synchronization of picture to narrative. A large proportion of the Carroll illustrations, eighteen of the thirty-eight, illustrate the same or almost the same moment in the story as does a Tenniel illustration. Another nine illustrate moments in the story that are fairly close to ones that Tenniel illustrated. The remaining eleven are unique to the Carroll manuscript; they lack counterparts in the published book.

Altogether, then, some three-quarters of the Carroll illustrations synchronize more or less closely with the Tenniel illustrations. Admittedly this agreement could result just from Carroll's authority over both projects; but that Tenniel actually studied the Carroll illustrations is apparent from some striking resemblances.

For example, the two illustrations that show Alice just after her fall into the pool of tears look very much alike (fig. 2.1 by Carroll; fig. 2.2 by Tenniel). Although Alice's facial expressions differ, neither her posture nor the observer's point

Fig. 2.1. Carroll. Alice in the pool of tears. From *Alice's Adventures under Ground.*

Fig. 2.2. Tenniel. Alice in the pool of tears. From *Alice's Adventures in Wonderland.*

of view changes much. What change there is involves a more closely observed realism of Alice's posture in the water. Despite the text, which describes Alice as "up to her chin in salt water," and also despite the law of gravity, Carroll's Alice floats with much of her body out of the water. But Tenniel's Alice has to exert herself to keep her chin above water, as would realistically be the case—even in salt water.

Other differences between these two images, including the difference in Alice's expression, follow from this basic physical difference. Carroll's Alice lifts her left arm high, in what looks to be as much a gesture of some sort as an athletic maneuver. But in Tenniel's picture the arm is closer to the water, about to stroke it. Tenniel also shows the other arm already engaged in the water; Carroll does not. The face of Carroll's Alice is perfectly composed, but the open mouth of Tenniel's Alice suggests breathlessness and alarm. The moods of the two pictures are quite different. Carroll's drawing is tranquil, even mysterious; Tenniel's approaches closer to panic.

A case can be made against Tenniel's naturalizing of this scene. Although the text justifies his showing Alice sunk deep in the water, nothing that Carroll wrote suggests that her response was a frantic one. (The sole remark that Alice "swam about, trying to find her way out," suggests diligence more than a life-and-death struggle.) Also, Carroll's serene if impossible picture is very attractive. Whichever image one prefers, however, it is obvious that Tenniel took Carroll's into account when he drew his own.

A less complex example is the relation between figures 2.3 and 2.4, Carroll's and Tenniel's renderings of Bill the Lizard being propelled from the chimney by Alice's foot. Tenniel has drawn a much more plausible lizard, improved upon Carroll's two chimneys and added some appropriate smoke. However, the angle of view is almost identical, and so is Bill's posture. It is apparent that Tenniel set out to draw in more accurate detail what Carroll had already drawn.

From early in his career, when he illustrated *Aesop's Fables* (1848), Tenniel gained a reputation for the skillful illustration of animals; he later acknowledged spending much time at the Zoological Gardens in London, making mental notes (not sketches) of how various animals actually looked.[7] This expertise may explain the major difference between Carroll's and Tenniel's drawings of Alice preparing to play croquet (figs. 2.5, 2.6). Carroll's Alice uses an ostrich for a croquet mallet, in keeping with the description given in the man-an illustrated book of natural history from the deanery at Christ Church, to improve the accuracy of his drawings. So far as I know, the particular book has not been identified; it may have been Thomas Bewick's well-known *General History of Quadrupeds* (1790, often reprinted), which contains illustrations of a jerboa and a guinea pig that approximate animals in one of Carroll's full-page drawings. It also includes a hedgehog illustration (fig. 2.7) that roughly anticipates Carroll's drawing and more closely anticipates Tenniel's (note especially the treatment of the right rear leg). Whether or not Carroll consulted the Bewick cut, Tenniel almost certainly did—besides consulting Carroll's drawing.[8]

Fig. 2.3. Carroll. Bill the Lizard. From *Alice's Adventures under Ground.*

Fig. 2.4. Tenniel. Bill the Lizard. From *Alice's Adventures in Wonderland.*

Fig. 2.5. Carroll. Alice at croquet. From *Alice's Adventures under Ground.*

uscript; but Tenniel's Alice holds a flamingo, which accords with a revision that Carroll made in the published text. Ostriches grow up to eight feet tall and weigh up to three hundred pounds—too much for a girl to hold in her arms! The revision is more realistic. If Carroll asked Tenniel to show Alice carrying an ostrich, Tenniel may have asked him to change the text to something more plausible—even as he later persuaded Carroll to drop the wasp-in-a-wig episode from *Through the Looking-Glass* (discussed in chapter 10).

However, aside from the difference in birds, figures 2.5 and 2.6 are alike to an extent that can hardly be accidental. In each picture, in front of a nondescript background, the girl and the bird face each other in profile or close to it; their general orientation in Tenniel's picture mirrors that in Carroll's. The hedgehog does not change its orientation, and hardly changes otherwise. Carroll is known to have borrowed

Fig. 2.6. Tenniel. Alice at croquet. From *Alice's Adventures in Wonderland.*

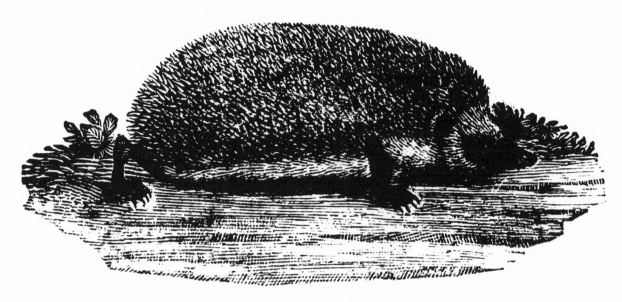

Fig. 2.7. Thomas Bewick. Hedgehog. From *A General History of Quadrupeds* (1790; rpt. 1791).

Fig. 2.8. Carroll. The Caterpillar and Alice. From *Alice's Adventures under Ground.*

Fig. 2.9. Tenniel. The Caterpillar and Alice. From *Alice's Adventures in Wonderland.*

Tenniel's drawing of Alice in conversation with the Caterpillar departs considerably from Carroll's (figs. 2.8, 2.9), but it still shows a dependence upon it. Tenniel depicts a slightly later moment, the start of chapter 5 rather than the end of chapter 4, where the Caterpillar was first glimpsed (as Carroll tried—unconvincingly—to show it) "with its arms folded." Tenniel's Caterpillar "at last . . . took the hookah out of its mouth, and addressed her in a languid, sleepy voice"—a moment of increased dramatic interest. Tenniel keeps the general scale of Carroll's drawing and makes only a minor change in the angle of view. That change is the necessary accompaniment to Tenniel's redeployment of the two figures, so that the Caterpillar is viewed almost from behind. By arranging the characters this way Tenniel is able to suggest, in trompe-l'oeil fashion, that the Caterpillar has a human face. The implied mouth, nose and brow arise from actual caterpillar feet seen in silhouette. The result is a mood of personification without the unconvincing explicitness of Carroll's version.[9] On this improved arrangement, Alice, if she is to face the Caterpillar, also must face the viewer, and vice versa; this requires the elevation of the point of view if Alice is not to be hidden entirely by the mushroom. Tenniel's Alice stands as the text describes her, "stretched . . . up on tiptoe," just "peep[ing] over the edge of the mushroom." Her expressive eyes are framed by the edge, and we can see them peering at the Caterpillar—a more striking arrangement than the one in Carroll's picture: Tenniel also improved the hookah—called for by the text—which Carroll had ineptly made into a pipe. In general, Tenniel's view of Alice and the Caterpillar recognizably derives from Carroll's, but it improves the realism and psychological interest of major details.

Carroll included in *Alice's Adventures under Ground* several full-page drawings, set sideways to the text, which mimic "plates" in a published book. The only full-page illustration in *Alice's Adventures in Wonderland* is the frontispiece—which will get separate discussion in the next chapter. Several of the *Under Ground* plates synchronize more or less closely with several of Tenniel's drawings; for example, the encounter of Alice with the Mouse in the pool of tears (figs. 2.10, 2.11), and the scene in which Alice grows too big for the little room (figs. 2.12, 2.13). The moments of figures 2.10 and 2.11 are slightly different: in figure 2.10 Alice is just greeting the Mouse, whereas in figure 2.11 their conversation has deteriorated to the point where Alice is talking "half to herself,"

and the Mouse is on his way out of the scene. Tenniel's drawing captures better than Carroll's the ultimately unsatisfactory nature of this encounter—not to mention the more accurate rendering of the Mouse buoyant in the water—but it copies the disposition of Alice's legs and arms very closely. The ornamental fish that Carroll added, Tenniel left out, perhaps as distracting.

Carroll's full-page illustration of Alice growing too large for the small room (fig. 2.12) has been praised, as compared to Tenniel's version (fig. 2.13), for more powerfully evoking fetal claustrophobia.[10] By placing Alice's foot and head at opposite corners of the picture frame, Carroll suggests that she has completely exhausted the available space—a suggestion absent from the Tenniel illustration, which does not show her feet. Tenniel shows the actual location of walls, floor and ceiling; that is a more realistic but less effective approach than Carroll's "naive" substitution of the picture frame for the physical structure of the room. Furthermore, by showing the actual room, Tenniel has occasion to show the window through which Alice thrusts her arm, in a first effort to escape her confinement; the moment here is slightly later than in the Carroll illustration, and the scene of confinement is less absolute. Despite these considerable differences, the basic composition and general proportions of the two pictures are much the same; this similarity is especially obvious if one is viewed in a mirror. Tenniel altered Carroll's drawing considerably, but he did not ignore it.

Carroll drew two consecutive illustrations that show, first, Alice swimming in the water with various birds and other creatures (fig. 2.14); and, then, Alice with one of the birds on the bank, dripping wet (fig. 2.15). Tenniel combined these two illustrations into one that shows Alice and all the creatures as "a queer-looking party . . . assembled on the bank—the birds with draggled feathers, the animals with their fur clinging close to them, and all dripping wet, cross, and uncomfortable" (fig. 2.16). Although it has been said that the picture unfortunately "shows everybody dry," Alice's hair and dress look wet enough, and the feathers on the parrot do seem "draggled."[11] Still, some puddles would improve the effect. The two crabs, not to be seen in Carroll's illustration, are included in this one because they have speaking roles later in the chapter. The monkey on the left, the owl in the middle, and the rodent-like animals on the right are all characters that are not mentioned in the text; they come from Carroll's illustration. By moving the group out of the

Fig. 2.10. Carroll. Alice and the Mouse in the pool of tears. From *Alice's Adventures under Ground*.

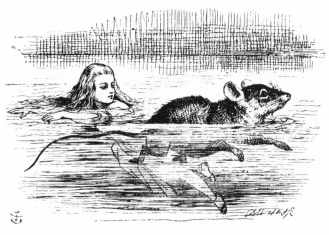

Fig. 2.11. Tenniel. Alice and the Mouse in the pool of tears. From *Alice's Adventures in Wonderland*.

Fig. 2.12. Carroll. Alice outgrowing the room. From *Alice's Adventures under Ground*.

Fig. 2.13. Tenniel. Alice outgrowing the room. From *Alice's Adventures in Wonderland*.

Fig. 2.14. Carroll. Alice swimming with the creatures. From *Alice's Adventures under Ground*.

Fig. 2.15. Carroll. Alice and a bird on the bank. From *Alice's Adventures under Ground*.

Fig. 2.16. Tenniel. Alice with the creatures on the bank. From *Alice's Adventures in Wonderland*.

Fig. 2.17. Carroll. The creatures fleeing from Alice. From *Alice's Adventures under Ground*.

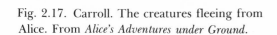

water onto dry land, Tenniel managed to show the creatures to better advantage; he also gave the illustration a motivation and a focus in the Mouse's recitation of English history.

From these examples and others that could be cited, it is clear that Tenniel was respectful of his pictorial source as well as of the text that he was illustrating. He departs selectively from Carroll's prototype, usually in the interests of greater realism. For a century readers have approved the way that Tenniel creates a realistic counterpart to the fantastic world that Carroll describes. In a few instances, as has already been remarked, the primitivism of Carroll's drawings hints at subtleties and sophistications more interesting for the modern reader than anything that Tenniel's literalism can express. And Tenniel, needing the space to illustrate the additions that Carroll made to the text of the published version, ignored some of Carroll's drawings, quite possibly on Carroll's own recommendation. One or two of these may be regretted, such as the poignant scene of Alice being left behind by the frightened creatures (fig. 2.17). But these are exceptional cases. By and large Tenniel improved, as he was supposed to do, upon the model presented by Carroll's illustrations for *Alice's Adventures under Ground.*

CHAPTER THREE

"Look at the Frontispiece"

"The judge, by the way, was the King, and as he wore his crown over the wig, (look at the frontispiece if you want to see how he did it,) he did not look at all comfortable, and it was certainly not becoming." Some readers, looking at the frontispiece to *Alice's Adventures in Wonderland* (fig. 3.1), have interpreted the King's odd countenance as showing anger at the Knave; but according to the text all that it shows is the King's awkward discomfort under his double burden. The self-absorption of the King contrasts to the other-directed emotion of the Queen beside him, who has a more personal reason to be angry at the Knave, and who shows her anger by glaring at him and crossing her arms defensively.[1]

The Knave, in his disgrace, is relegated to the inferior half of this carefully bisected picture. The smug expression on his face has no textual authority; Carroll does not even establish that the Knave is guilty as charged, let alone that he is unrepentant. The red nose (indicated by hatching in the original black-and-white engraving, and actually colored red in *The Nursery "Alice"* [1890]) is not mentioned in the text either. Nonetheless, the red nose does have a textual explanation: the Duchess's cook testifies, under cross-examination, that tarts are made of "pepper, mostly." The pepper-box that she carries with her to the trial makes bystanders sneeze; evidently the pepper tarts had the same effect on the thieving Knave. To be red-nosed in this case is to be red-handed: guilty. It is in keeping with the rest of the Knave's disorderly trial that no one notices this incriminating evidence, as plain as the nose on his face.[2]

The Knave shares the lower half of the picture with two guards, several bird-barristers seated at a table, and an expectant executioner lurking in the background. Carroll does mention two guards, but not any barristers—the King, the Queen, and some jurymen ask all the questions—nor any executioner. Conversely, Tenniel ignores the background details of the scene that Carroll describes at the start of chapter 11:

> The King and Queen of Hearts were seated on their throne when they [Alice and the Gryphon] arrived, with a great crowd assembled about them—all sorts of little birds and beasts, as well as the whole pack of cards: the Knave was standing before them, in chains, with a soldier on each side to guard him; and near the King was the White Rabbit, with a trumpet in one hand, and a scroll of parchment in the other. In the very middle of the court was a table, with a large dish of tarts upon it.

The beginning of this passage better describes Carroll's own illustration of the scene (fig. 3.2) than Tenniel's.

All that is missing from Carroll's illustration are the two guards, who in fact were not mentioned in the briefer manuscript account: "The King and Queen were seated on their throne when they arrived, with a great crowd assembled around them: the Knave was in custody: and before the King stood the white rabbit, with a trumpet in one hand, and a scroll of parchment in the other." Here Carroll did not specify, either, that the "great crowd" includes "all sorts of little birds and beasts"; these figures appeared for the first time in figure 3.2, Carroll's manuscript illustration—which in turn served as the basis for the amplified description that Carroll finally wrote for *Alice's Adventures*. In illustrating this new scene, Tenniel ignored the crowd altogether. Not only would it have cluttered up the picture, but it would have required space, and space is scarce in this boldly foreshortened picture. Except for the pasteboard body of the Knave and the flat face of the uncomfortably stiff King, the individual characters are plausibly three-dimensional; and yet the total picture space is very shallow. Tenniel most obviously foreshortened the runway or platform on which the White Rabbit is standing; it seems to be hardly as wide as he is.

The text of the manuscript version makes no mention of any larger background for the trial, and Carroll's illustration seems to be set indifferently out of doors. But the published text sets the trial in a "court" with a "roof," and the compression that Tenniel brings to the scene befits this indoor setting.

By minimizing depth Tenniel draws attention to the two-

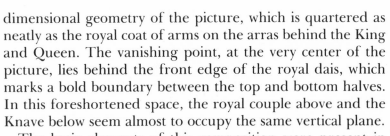

Fig. 3.1. Tenniel. Trial scene. Frontispiece to *Alice's Adventures in Wonderland*.

Fig. 3.2. Carroll. Trial scene. From *Alice's Adventures under Ground*.

dimensional geometry of the picture, which is quartered as neatly as the royal coat of arms on the arras behind the King and Queen. The vanishing point, at the very center of the picture, lies behind the front edge of the royal dais, which marks a bold boundary between the top and bottom halves. In this foreshortened space, the royal couple above and the Knave below seem almost to occupy the same vertical plane.

The basic elements of this composition were present in Carroll's drawing; Tenniel intensified them by suppressing the third dimension (and the crowd with it), and by not letting the top and bottom halves of the scene overlap. He also reversed the positions of the King and Queen, giving a diagonal force to the Queen's baleful glare at the Knave.

There is a slight difference in the timing of these two pictures. In Tenniel's version the White Rabbit is reading the accusation (the first half of the nursery rhyme "The Queen of Hearts"). For the manuscript version, Carroll had chosen a less important moment just before, when the White Rabbit gives a preliminary flourish on his trumpet. Tenniel showed that moment too, fixing it in a small but very popular drawing (fig. 3.3). There is no reason in the text why the White Rabbit's trumpet should be so tiny as it is in figures 3.1 and 3.3; it may be that Tenniel was playing a private joke, parodying Carroll's clumsily exaggerated drawing of the trumpet in figure 3.2.

of a Horse" (fig. 3.5). Other resemblances suggest that Tenniel consulted this engraving: the owl and the King look alike; also the lion and the Queen; and the dog and the Knave.[3] Furthermore, Bennett's picture is organized in the same tight space as Tenniel's, and it too is divided in half horizontally. One of Bennett's four barristers has the hooked beak of a bird of prey, as does one of Tenniel's. Tenniel took this joke against the legal profession one step further by making the most prominent of the barristers a veritable parrot of the law. (There may also be another, private joke involved, for in chapters 2 and 3 an eaglet and a lory—that is, parrot—represent Alice Liddell's two sisters, Edith and Lorina.) When Tenniel drew a later illustration of this same scene

Fig. 3.3 Tenniel. The White Rabbit. From *Alice's Adventures in Wonderland.*

Tenniel supplies a table, as does Carroll, and outfits it with tarts that look more like tarts and less like cupcakes. The birds sitting at the table—three bewigged barristers on the right and at least two (judging from a later illustration, figure 3.4) on the left—are not called for in the text. They may descend from the bewigged dog and birds in an enigmatic frontispiece by Tenniel's friend, Charles H. Bennett, depicting "Man tried at the Court of the Lion for the ill-treatment

Fig. 3.4. Tenniel. The Knave on trial. From *Alice's Adventures in Wonderland.*

Fig. 3.5. Charles H. Bennett. "Man tried at the Court of the Lion." From
The Fables of Aesop and Others, Translated into Human Nature (1857; rpt.
1875).

(fig. 3.4), he showed all the barristers nodding, indifferent to the defendant's fate.

The most curious prototype for the *Wonderland* frontispiece is Tenniel's own illustration to Martin Tupper's poem "Of Estimating Character" (fig. 3.6), one of the several that he did for the illustrated edition of Tupper's uplifting *Proverbial Philosophy* (1854).[4] This drawing was engraved by the Brothers Dalziel, who later engraved all the *Alice* illustrations.

The passage that this particular engraving illustrates has to do with the murder trial of a man who killed impulsively after repeated insults and provocations. Society ("man") judges this act to be a capital offense; but God ("the Righteous Judge") knows that the deed is less guilty than the conduct of the victim who maliciously provoked it. Tenniel's illustration of this little homily on the deficiency of human justice shows an arrangement much like that of the frontispiece to *Alice's Adventures*, with the judge occupying the upper half of the picture, and the defendant in chains (like the Knave) at the lower left, in right profile, his head held back and his arms held high. The court's evidence of the evil deed rests on a cloth-covered table before him, as in the frontispiece; and an eager executioner loiters on the scene—though not in the background.[5] The young scribe on the judge's left prefigures the White Rabbit. The close, foreshortened space of this scene of judgment is essentially the same as in the frontispiece. A major difference is in the demeanor of the defendant, who here pleads for mercy (to an indifferent court), unlike the Knave, who is complacent in his sins. The troubled gaze of the youth shows that he, like Tupper, views the scene with greater misgiving than the rest of the court, and feels an unexpected compassion for death's next victim. Unlike Wonderland, this is not a world where every arbitrary judgment entails an arbitrary pardon.

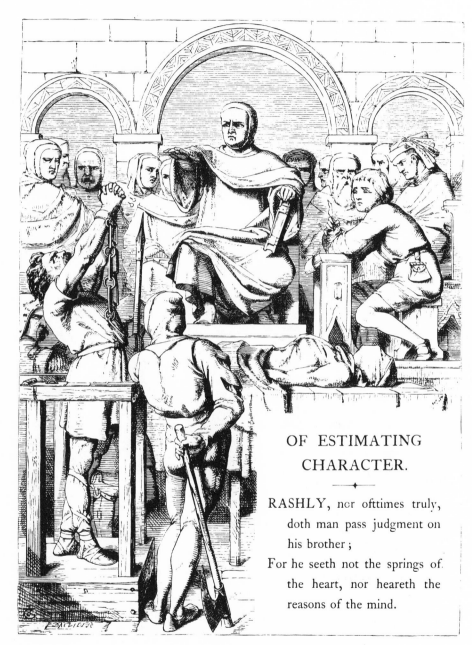

OF ESTIMATING CHARACTER.

RASHLY, nor ofttimes truly, doth man pass judgment on his brother; For he seeth not the springs of the heart, nor heareth the reasons of the mind.

Fig. 3.6. Tenniel. "Of Estimating Character." From Martin F. Tupper, *Proverbial Phiolosophy: Illustrated* (1854; rpt. n.d.).

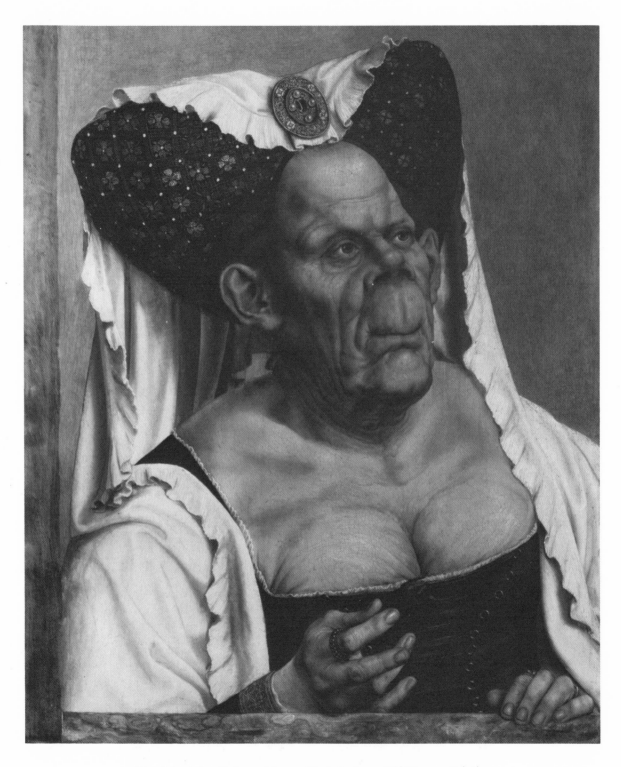

Fig. 4.1. After Quinten Massys (?). *A Grotesque Old Woman*. Painting.
Reproduced by courtesy of the Trustees, The National Gallery. London.

CHAPTER FOUR

The Lineage of the Ugly Duchess

Early in 1920 Christie's, the London auction house, sold a painting of a grotesque old woman which they described as a "Portrait of the Duchess of Carinthia and Tyrol, in jewelled head-dress," and which they attributed to the sixteenth-century Flemish artist Quintin Matsys (fig. 4.1; the name has also been spelled Quentin Matsys, Quentin Metsys, and Quinten Massys—now the preferred spelling). Later that year the popular *Illustrated London News* devoted a two-page spread to the painting, including a full-page reproduction. The article, by William A. Baillie-Grohman, had the eye-catching headline "The Ugliest Woman in History." Over the illustration was a headline almost as remarkable, at least for readers of *Alice*: "Tenniel's Model for the Duchess in 'Alice': The Ugliest Woman." The long caption below the painting repeated this claim: "The portrait has . . . interest as having been the original from which Sir John Tenniel drew the familiar and hideous countenance of the Duchess in his illustrations to 'Alice in Wonderland' " (figs. 4.2, 4.3).[1]

Fig. 4.3. Tenniel. Alice and the Duchess. From *Alice's Adventures in Wonderland*.

Fig. 4.2. Tenniel. The Duchess. From *Alice's Adventures in Wonderland*.

In the article proper, Baillie-Grohman did not mention Tenniel; indeed he had little to say about the painting, mainly confining himself to the scandalous biography of the supposed subject. Baillie-Grohman was doubly qualified to discuss the portrait, for he was a connoisseur of some prestige, and also a frequent chronicler of "Tyrol and the Tyrolese"—the title that he gave his first book, published forty-five years earlier. In his more recent book *The Land in the Mountains* (1907), Baillie-Grohman had devoted eight pages to the Duchess Margaret (1318–1369), who was nicknamed "Maultasche"—usually rendered "pocket-mouthed." He commented, with some regret, "Of the truth of the legends relating to the monstrously ill-shaped mouth of Margaret, we have no means of judging, for there is no contemporary portrait of her in existence."[2] In this book Baillie-Grohman noted another explanation for the nickname, according to which it meant a box on the ears—alluding to a family incident with political consequences. And in the *Illustrated London News* article he preferred that explanation. Nonetheless, in the article he did mention "her fame as the ugliest woman of her day." Presumably the newly found portrait substantiated that reputation—though indirectly, since it was painted over a hundred years after her death.

Baillie-Grohman next wrote a more scholarly article for the art journal *Burlington Magazine*, in which he discussed the painting itself in some detail. He now emphasized an aspect that had only been mentioned before: the painting closely resembled a drawing in the collection of Windsor Castle that had been attributed to Leonardo (fig. 4.4). Baillie-Grohman concluded that Tenniel "must . . . have been acquainted with one or the other"—the painting or the drawing—"when he drew his famous Duchess in 'Alice in Wonderland.' " Perhaps Tenniel had seen the painting "in the collection of Alfred Seymour," the father of the woman from whose estate Christie's had sold it.[3]

Eleven years later, in his centennial biography of Carroll, Langford Reed repeated the original claim, without mentioning Leonardo. Opposite a plate reproducing the painting, he remarked, "For his studies of the Duchess [Tenniel] took as his model the famous portrait of the hideous Duchess of Corinthia [sic] and Tyrol, painted about the year 1520 by the Flemish artist, Quentin Metsys." In a footnote he referred to *The Ugly Duchess*, a recent historical novel that Lion Feuchtwanger had based on Margaret's life. First published in Germany as *Die hässliche Herzogin Margarete Maultasch* (1926), the novel appeared in English translation two years later. It was under the influence of its English title that the Carroll-Tenniel character would gradually come to be known as "the Ugly Duchess." Carroll simply called her "the Duchess."[4]

In her still useful critical biography of Carroll, published in 1945, Florence Becker Lennon thought the painting a more likely source than the drawing, because Tenniel "uses the detail of costume in that painting."[5] In his popular edition, *The Annotated Alice* (1960), Martin Gardner cited the painting only—which he called "the portrait of the *Ugly Duchess*."[6] Meanwhile, the painting had passed into the collection of the National Gallery, London, where it was catalogued by Martin Davies in 1955.[7]

Davies doubts that Massys himself painted the work (he thinks it is a copy after a painting by Massys now lost), and he rejects the supposed connection to the duchess Margaret. Taking up the question whether Tenniel had used the painting as a source, he suggests that besides the painting there are other possibilities just as plausible: (1) other painted versions; (2) the Windsor drawing; (3) an early nineteenth-century engraving after the Windsor drawing; and (4) various seventeeth- and eighteenth-century engravings of a similar subject.

Davies thinks that the lost Massys original had probably been modeled after the Windsor Castle drawing—or rather after the original of the Windsor Castle drawing, itself judged to be a copy. Massys would have supplied the additional details of costume, most obviously the embroidery in the headdress.

In this respect Davies follows Kenneth Clark, formerly director of the National Gallery, who attributes the Windsor Castle drawing to Francesco Melzi, a pupil of Leonardo's.[8] As regards subject matter, Clark sees no reason to believe that either the drawing or the painting represented the Duchess Margaret. "The tradition to this effect is of no antiquity," he remarks, citing by way of contrast a "free engraving" of the picture by the seventeenth-century artist Wenzel Hollar, in which the corresponding figure is identified as the Queen of Tunis (fig. 4.5). Davies, dismissing both alternatives as equally fanciful, simply entitles the painting *A Grotesque Old Woman*. This new title is an adaptation from the earliest published reference to the painting, made by Gustav Waagen in 1854, a decade before Tenniel prepared his drawings. ("The great art-critic, Waagen," as Carroll called him in a different context.[9])

Davies doubts a proposal by Erwin Panofsky, according to which the Leonardesque drawing did not represent any actual woman, but rather was a general satire on lascivious old women, in the tradition of Erasmus's *Praise of Folly*. The question of Leonardo's purposes in sketching his many grotesque portraits or caricatures, including others similar to the original of the Windsor Castle drawing, has engaged art

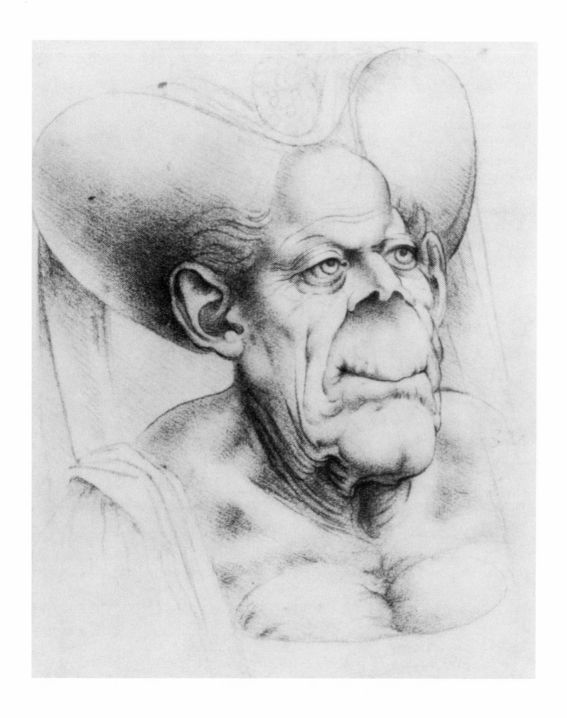

Fig. 4.4. Francisco Melzi, after Leonardo da Vinci. Head and shoulders of
a hideous old woman. Drawing. Copyright reserved. Reproduced by gra-
cious permission of Her Majesty Queen Elizabeth II.

historians from Vasari on down to Ernst Gombrich, and is beyond the scope of this discussion.[10] Massys's intentions for his painting likewise remain uncertain.

Of the various possible sources that Davies mentions for the Tenniel illustrations, not all seem equally probable. He of course mentions the Windsor drawing; and also an engraving, published in 1806, which represents it in accurate detail. He might also have mentioned a faithfully-drawn copy of the Windsor drawing, now in the Spencer Collection of the New York Public Library.[11] But all of these images lack the detailed treatment of the headdress (cruciform floral embroidery) that characterizes both the painting and Tenniel's two illustrations. It was on this ground that Lennon favored the painting as a likely source, rather than the Windsor drawing. A similar point can be made about the treatment of the woman's hair. In the Windsor drawing and its copies, the hair at the temples is wispy; but in the painting it has a wave; and in the Tenniel illustrations it has been obviously crimped. Tenniel elaborated a hint of vanity from the painting that is not in any of the versions of the Windsor drawing.[12]

The Hollar engraving (fig. 4.5) is in the tradition of the painting, not the drawing; the headdress is embroidered, and the treatment of the hands also conforms to that of the painting. But in size and in detail the headdress is emphasized less in the engraving than in the painting, which makes it a less likely source for Tenniel.

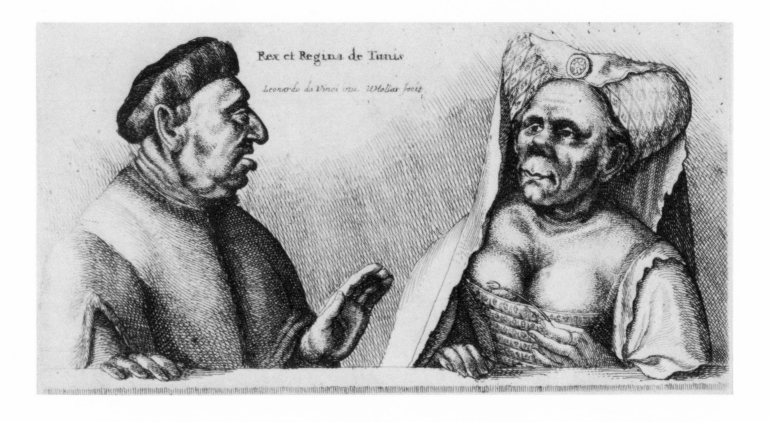

Fig. 4.5. Wenzel Hollar. *Rex et Regina de Tunis*. Engraving. Reproduced by permission of the British Museum.

Marguerite surnommée Maltasche, c'est-à-dire, Gueule de Sac étoit fille de Henri X.º du nom Duc de Carinthie, Comte de Tirol ensuite Roi de Bohême mort en 1331, et d'Anne fille de Wenceslas IV surnommé le Bon Roi de Bohême. Elle nâquit en 1300 et après la mort de son Pere, ayant eu en partage le Comté de Tirol, elle epousa en premieres noces en 1329 Jean Henri Duc de Moravie frere de l'Empereur Charles IV. dont elle se separa en 1341. L'année suivante 1342 elle epousa en secondes noces Louis fils de l'Empereur Louis de Baviere qui mourut en 1361. De son second mariage elle n'eut qu'un fils nommé Maynard IV dernier Comte de Tirol né en 1344 et qui epousa à 14 ans Marguerite fille de l'Empereur Albert II dont il n'eut point d'enfans. Maynard IV étant mort en 1363, Marguerite Maltasche sa mere céda l'année suivante 1364 le Comté de Tirol à la Maison d'Autriche. Elle mourut en 1366.

Fig. 4.6. Gilles-Antoine Demarteau. "Marguerite surnommée Maltasche."
Engraving. Phot. Bibl. nat. Paris.

In her monograph on Massys, Andrée de Bosque reproduces two French engravings of the painting (or paintings), one engraved by Gilles-Antoine Demarteau (1750–1802) and the other by Ephraïm Conquy (1809–43). The first identifies the sitter as "Marguerite surnommée Maltasche." This tradition of identification, which probably influenced the cataloguer for the Christie's sale, was apparently French; and as early as 1879 a French connoisseur dissented from it.[13] Of the two engravings, the Demarteau is closer both to the National Gallery painting and to the Tenniel illustration, especially as regards the embroidery of the headdress (fig. 4.6). Assuming that Tenniel had access to a copy of the engraving, it could have served him for a model as well as the painting.

The question remains whether Tenniel might have had access to the painting itself. Lennon follows Baillie-Grohman in suggesting that Tenniel saw it in the collection of Alfred Seymour; but according to Davies, Alfred did not inherit it from his brother, Henry Danby Seymour, until 1877. Waagen reports having seen it in the older brother's collection in London in 1850. Might Tenniel have seen it there some fifteen years later?

There is a possible connection. Henry Danby Seymour, like Dodgson, studied at Christ Church, Oxford. He graduated in 1842, eight years before Dodgson matriculated, so they were not contemporaries.[14] But a classmate of Seymour's, John Ruskin, became acquainted with Carroll in the late fifties, both still having rooms in Christ Church. And there are records from the seventies of Ruskin's advising Carroll on illustrating his later books.

During their undergraduate years, Ruskin and Seymour socialized often.[15] Given the young Ruskin's interest in painting, it is likely that he knew Seymour's respectable collection. There is no record of contact between Seymour and Ruskin (let alone Carroll) in the sixties, but Seymour's standing as a member of parliament would not have made such contact unlikely.

The overlapping associations of Seymour, Ruskin, Carroll, and Tenniel may have resulted in Tenniel's consulting Seymour's painting, by different traditions supposed to represent either "a frightful old woman" (Waagen's phrase) or a particular ugly duchess, as a detailed model for his own duchess, who is described in the text simply as being "*very* ugly" (p. 132). The most likely alternative source is the Demarteau engraving. Whichever the source was, Tenniel may have intended a reference to the tradition of the ugly duchess Margaret Maultasche.

Of course, Tenniel mitigates the grotesqueness of the tradition. He replaces the emblematic rose in the Duchess's hand with a sprawling baby, who covers up any immodest neckline. Carroll would have disliked the sexual satire of the Massys painting, and Tenniel managed to make little of it. Instead, he drew attention to the Duchess's remarkable headdress.

In his apprenticeship years, Tenniel closely studied medieval costume, and that interest enlivened many of the minor drawings that he produced during his early years on the staff of *Punch*.[16] Especially at the start Tenniel did many ornamental initials, a neomedieval form of illustration that invited the use of medieval motifs. Two of these initials use elaborate women's headdresses to shape the capital letter *M* (figs. 4.7, 4.8). When Tenniel illustrated, and perhaps wrote, the series called "Punch's Book of British Costumes," which ran in 1860, he used the same calligraphic device (fig. 4.9). This drawing carries a joke caption, but the drawing itself hardly exaggerates its prototype, a fifteenth-century monumental effigy.[17] Contemporary writers had ridiculed the extravagance of such headdresses, and nineteeth-century historians renewed the ridicule. The author of this chapter in the *Punch* series refers to old jokes about them, "mostly far too coarse to quote"—probably about horns and cuckoldry.

In his *History of Caricature & Grotesque in Literature and Art*, chapters of which first appeared in the prestigious *Art-Journal*, the antiquarian Thomas Wright cited one such headdress as typifying the extravagance of late medieval costume. The record of this headdress was a fifteenth-century misericord from Shropshire, which Wright reproduced as drawn and engraved by F. W. Fairholt (fig. 4.10).[18] Panofsky later used this illustration to document the satirical tradition in which he would place the Massys painting. Possibly the Fairholt engraving has a more direct relation to Tenniel's Duchess. In the frontal aspect of the face, and certain details of the nose and chin, it more closely resembles Tenniel's Duchess than the Massys portrait does. Given its subject matter, Tenniel would almost certainly have seen, perhaps owned, a copy of Wright's work. It is likely that Tenniel's ugly Duchess reflects aspects of both the Massys painting and the Fairholt engraving.

Fig. 4.7. Tenniel. Woman in medieval headdress. From *Punch*, January–June 1852.

Fig. 4.8. Tenniel. Woman in medieval headdress. From *Punch*, 28 July 1856.

Fig. 4.9. Tenniel. Woman in medieval headdress. From *Punch*, 3 November 1860.

Fig. 4.10. F. W. Fairholt. Misericord: woman in medieval headdress. From Thomas Wright, *A History of Caricature & the Grotesque in Literature and Art* (1865).

CHAPTER FIVE

Sign of Madness: Shakespeare to Tenniel

The Nursery "Alice" (1890), which Lewis Carroll wrote specifically for "Children aged from Nought to Five," is not only simpler in its plot and language than *Alice's Adventures in Wonderland* (1866), on which it is based; it also emphasizes the illustrations more. They are enlarged, even more than the pages are, and colored; furthermore, Carroll repeatedly draws attention to them in the text. Occasionally he glosses some detail of illustration that he thinks might be difficult for young readers, as when he comments on Tenniel's depiction of the March Hare at the mad tea party (fig. 5.1): "That's the March Hare, with the long ears, and straws mixed up with his hair. The straws showed he was mad—I don't know why."[1]

This chapter will confirm Carroll's observation that the straws showed that the March Hare was mad (many readers miss this point), and it will also review some of the history of this signification.

The straw was probably Tenniel's idea, not Carroll's, even though Tenniel drew all the illustrations for *Alice* on commission from Carroll and under his supervision. The device had served as a conventional sign of madness in many illustrations drawn for *Punch* before and during Tenniel's employment on the art staff there; indeed, Tenniel had drawn quite a few of these illustrations himself. The use of this detail in the mad tea-party illustration was probably a routine embellishment by the artist.

The first of the many *Punch* drawings to use the sign, possibly drawn by H. G. Hine or Hablot Browne, appeared in the first of the series of "almanacks" that *Punch* published, the one for 1842—eight years before Tenniel joined the staff. At the top of the page devoted to March is a drawing titled "Maniac March Hares" (fig. 5.2). The hare in the center, wearing a dress, is strewing flowers from the basket held in her right hand; and she is crowned with wisps of straw.

The general mad-hare motif for March is introduced by the *Almanack* entry for the last day of February, on the pre-

Fig. 5.1. Tenniel. March Hare at tea party. From *Alice's Adventures in Wonderland.*

vious page: "HARE-HUNTING ENDS, and Hares run mad for joy." (A euphemistic account of the rutting season.) *Almanack* entries for other days in March continue the theme; for example, 7 March, "The Society for the Prevention of Cruelty to Animals proposes to erect a Lunatic Asylum for insane hares." Lewis Carroll was only ten years old when this *Almanack* was published; given his interest in comic magazines, it may be that he came across it later, and that the personified maniac March hares there contributed to his mad tea party.

The central hare in the illustration—a madwoman strewing flowers and crowned with weeds—recalls the best-known madwoman in English literature. When Ophelia strews rosemary, fennel, columbines, and rue there is no mention in the text that she is crowned with wild plants (*Hamlet* IV.v), but Gertrude later describes her, at the time of her death, as carrying "fantastic garlands" and "coronet weeds" (IV.vii). Hence Rowe's influential stage direction for the earlier mad

MANIAC MARCH HARES.

Fig. 5.2. "Maniac March Hares." From *Punch*, Almanack for 1842.

scene: "Enter Ophelia, fantastically drest with Straws and Flowers" (1709; perpetuated by later editors). Benjamin West, in the scene he painted for John Boydell's Shakespeare Gallery, took care to include a few wisps of straw in Ophelia's hair (figure 5.3, a detail of the engraving after West by Francis Legat).[2]

The second *Punch* illustration to be considered here was done by Tenniel himself—it bears his monogram—within a year or so of his joining the *Punch* staff. It is an initial letter *C*, which introduces a letter supposedly written by "An English Dramatist" who specialized in aping contemporary French theatrical fashions. (By his own account, the opening of one of his plays coincided with the irreparable cracking of "the statue of SHAKESPEARE over Drury Lane portico.") He proposes a crazy scheme of simultaneous translation in which the French text of a play would be spoken aloud by the prompter, and translated into English by the actors on stage.[3]

The Tenniel illustration that introduces this nonsense shows an old man in a dressing gown and slippers, riding an umbrella for a hobbyhorse, crowned with straw, and holding a clutch of straws for a scepter (fig. 5.4). The hints of royal regalia, the offhand dress, the man's grizzled old age and his distracted yet dignified air suggest a version of King Lear, especially next to a paragraph that mentions Shakespeare. This particular image evidently derives from figure 5.5, a portrait engraving of Lear "after a study by Sir Joshua Reynolds," which appeared in Charles Knight's *Pictorial Edi-*

tion of the Works of Shakspere (1839–43, often reprinted); there may also be an element or two borrowed from the James Barry illustration for Boydell's Shakespeare Gallery (figure 5.6, a detail from the engraving after Barry by Legat).[4]

These earlier images of Lear lack both the crown of straw and the scepter supplied by Tenniel; and when Cordelia describes the mad Lear she does not mention any scepter; but her account of Lear's crown is famous:

> Crown'd with rank fumiter, and furrow-weeds,
> With hardocks, hemlock, nettles, cuckoo-flowers,
> Darnel, and all the idle weeds that grow
> In our sustaining corn.
>   [IV.iv.]

Evidently in theatrical performance this crown might be made entirely of straw; Garrick, at least, seems to have worn a "crown of straw." And a stage convention before Garrick's time gave the actor playing Lear a "straw scepter." As a young man, Tenniel frequented the London theaters, accompanied by his sketchbook; he probably knew such conventions at first hand.[5] In any case figure 5.4 does caricature Shakespeare's King Lear, even as it looks forward to Carroll's March Hare.

Four years later Tenniel produced several dozen cartoons for *Punch* under the general title "Punch's Illustrations to Shakespeare." The cartoons are unsigned, like much of Tenniel's early work for *Punch*; but the style obviously continues from the signed work of 1850 and 1851.[6] This series, which during its run appeared almost every week, satirized

Fig. 5.3. Francis Legat, after Benjamin West. "*Hamlet.* Act IV. Scene V." Engraving (detail). From *Collection of Prints, from Pictures Painted for the Purpose of Illustrating the Dramatic Works of Shakespeare* (1803). By permission of Weyerhaeuser Library, Macalester College, St. Paul, Minnesota.

Fig. 5.4. Tenniel. King Lear. From *Punch*, January–June 1851.

Fig. 5.5. After Sir Joshua Reynolds.
King Lear. From *Pictorial Edition of the
Works of Shakspere*, ed. Charles Knight
(n.d.).

Fig. 5.6. Francis Legat, after James Barry. "*King Lear*. Act V.
Scene III." Engraving (detail). From *Collection of Prints, from Pictures
Painted for the Purpose of Illustrating the Dramatic Works of Shakespeare* (1803).
By permission of Weyerhaeuser Library, Macalester College, St. Paul,
Minnesota.

the persistent vogue for pious illustrations of brief excerpts from Shakespeare's plays. Instead of ornamenting the text in the usual manner, Tenniel's illustrations subvert it by playing on some punning sense. The gag for each cartoon may have been concocted by the *Punch* editorial staff, even as they later supplied Tenniel with the ideas for his political cartoons. It is also possible, given Tenniel's early familiarity with the theater, that he framed the puns himself.

Tenniel's only illustration for *King Lear* in this series glosses a remark made by Edgar while impersonating the mad Tom o' Bedlam: "Poor Tom's a-cold." Construing this to mean not that Tom is cold but that he *has* a cold, Tenniel shows a madman (crowned in straw, with a straw-wrapped staff near at hand) trying to cure his cold in a crazy fashion (fig. 5.7; 13 October 1855). The gruel and hot water are conventional treatments, but applied unconventionally. Pre-

Fig. 5.7. Tenniel. "Poor Tom's a-cold." From *Punch*, 13 October 1855.

sumably Tom rubs a candle against his sinuses because he remembers but misunderstands a snatch from the old ballad "Waly, Waly," on the subject of "love": "But when 'tis auld it *waxeth cauld*, / And fades awa' like morning dew."

When Edgar plans his Tom-o'-Bedlam disguise he says only that he will "elf all [his] hair in knots" (*Lear* II.iii); but in the frontispiece to Rowe's edition his hair is also decked out with weeds and flowers. Benjamin West crowned Tom with weeds in his painting of the heath scene for Boydell's Shakespeare Gallery. Of course the role of Tom o' Bedlam was a conventional one when Edgar adopted it: sane beggars would pretend to be mad refugees from Bethlehem Hospital, so as to encourage charity. And it may be that even before the theatrical tradition of *King Lear*, weedy hair was a conventional sign of the madman—or of the feigned madman.[7]

Hamlet provided two texts for Tenniel's "Illustrations," one of them being a line from Ophelia's mad scene, "There's fennel for you, and columbines." Tenniel's mad Ophelia has herbs in her hand and ferns in the folds of her gown—not to mention straw in her hair (fig. 5.8; 17 November 1855). But instead of passing out the herbs when she says this line she gestures with them toward the scene she is commenting upon; and what she points out are three dancers from English pantomime, each impersonating the inamorata Columbine; they are busy flattering Claudius. (As early Shakespearean commentators had pointed out, fennel was a traditional emblem of flattery.)

Shakespeare did not invent all the madmen caricatured in *Punch*; the weekly news turned up others. John Leech and other staff cartoonists showed the likes of the pacifist John Bright, striking cabdrivers, and even the newly "cracked" Big Ben (the great bell of the Palace of Westminster) as crowned with straw. Figure 5.9 is one of two Tenniel cartoons showing Czar Nicholas I as insane at the time of the Crimean War. In the other he is shown as a mad dog. Both use the straw device.[8]

That device was a standard weapon in political caricature well before the founding of *Punch* in 1841. Rowlandson, for example, had shown Fox reduced to insanity by the fall of the Coalition (fig. 5.10); besides the straitjacket there is straw in his hair, and the attending doctor is the director of "Bedlam" (Bethlehem Hospital for the insane). In another cartoon Rowlandson shows another Bedlamite, Edmund Burke, about to be crowned with straw by a madwoman, herself crowned with straw.[9] Because pallets made of straw were

Fig. 5.8. Tenniel. "There's fennel for you, and columbines." From *Punch*, 17 November 1855.

Fig. 5.9. Tenniel. Czar Nicholas I. From *Punch*, January–June 1854.

common in Bedlam, the word "straw" became associated with madness. Pope refers to "the straw where Bedlam's prophet nods" (*Dunciad* 3:7); and Dr. Johnson spoke of "condemning" someone "to straw," meaning consigning them to the madhouse (*OED*). Hogarth's famous view of Bedlam in *The Rake's Progress* (1735) shows straw used as bedding and also as two kinds of headdress. In figure 5.11, a detail of the engraving, the naked megalomaniac seen through the door has woven straw into the shape of a crown; and the kneeling man in front of him has supplied his shaved head with a makeshift straw wig under his hat.[10] When George Cruikshank drew an engraving, "Jack Sheppard visits his Mother in Bedlam," for W. Harrison Ainsworth's popular novel *Jack Sheppard* (1839), he followed tradition by putting her on a bed of straw, with straw on her head (fig. 5. 12).[11]

Shakespeare's Edgar, in his role of "poor Tom," pretends to be a refugee from Bedlam; but the mad Lear and Cordelia, when they crown themselves with weeds, evoke a different context of associations. Madhouses exist within a culture; but from the Middle Ages to the Renaissance it was widely believed, especially in northern Europe, that there existed outside of culture, as a kind of antithesis to it, a race of wild men. These wholly uncivilized creatures, the spiritual descendants of the mad King Nebuchadnezzar, were often pictured wearing wreaths of wild plants on their heads—as in the example of figure 5.13, a German engraving from the late fifteenth century. It is possible that Shakespeare intended the mad Lear to revert to this traditional antitype of cultured man, though the tradition was never as strong in England as it was in the rest of northern Europe.[12]

Fig. 5.10. Thomas Rowlandson. *The Incurable*. Engraving. By permission of the British Museum.

Fig. 5.11. (opposite). William Hogarth. "*Madness, Thou Chaos of the Brain.*" Engraving (detail). From *The Rake's Progress* in *The Original and Genuine Works of William Hogarth* (1836). Yale Center for British Art, Paul Mellon collection.

Fig. 5.12. George Cruikshank. "Jack Sheppard visits his Mother in Bedlam." From W. Harrison Ainsworth, *Jack Sheppard* (1839; rpt. 1854).

The freshly-picked weeds of Lear and Ophelia seem quite different from the dead straw of Bedlam, though Garrick apparently found straw a more practical prop for the theater. In any case by the start of the nineteenth century the two emblems, and the two kinds of madness, had reduced to one. For Tenniel, straw in the hair simply meant that a character was mad.

The sign seems to have lost currency not long after Tenniel drew illustrations for *Alice's Adventures*. I don't know that any examples can be found in *Punch* after 1870. When other artists illustrated *Alice's Adventures* on the expiration of the copyright in 1907, some followed Tenniel's prototype illustrations closely enough to retain the straw device for the

March Hare; but a sampling suggests that most did not. Arthur Rackham is one well-known artist who omitted the straw; he may have thought that the sign had become obsolete, or possibly he did not know that it *was* a sign.

The most telling vestige of the tradition, precisely because it is so obviously vestigial, is the revision of Tenniel's March Hare that the Disney studios made for their animated version of *Alice*, released in 1951. On the top of the March Hare's head there is a definite patch of yellow something; but the viewer would be hard put to say what exactly it was; it might as well be fur as straw (fig. 5.14). If few viewers can tell what that yellow patch is supposed to be, not many will know (in Carroll's words) what it "showed," let alone "why."

Fig. 5.13. Martin Schongauer. *Wild Man Holding Shield with a Greyhound*. Engraving. National Gallery of Art, Washington, Rosenwald Collection.

Fig. 5.14. Walt Disney. March Hare at tea party. From *Alice in Wonderland*.
© 1951 Walt Disney Productions.

CHAPTER SIX

Alice and the Queen of Spades

"The Queen turned crimson with fury, and, after glaring at her for a moment like a wild beast, began screaming, 'Off with her head! Off—' " In the early editions of *Alice's Adventures in Wonderland* this sentence is all the text there is on page 117, where it appears directly below figure 6.1, as much a caption to that picture as a continuation of the story.[1] Looking up from the caption the reader will focus at least some attention on the tip of the Queen's outstretched index finger, partly because the gesture of pointing conventionally commands attention, but also because Tenniel has centered the whole composition of the picture on this point. The Queen who stands behind this threatening gesture takes up roughly a quarter of the picture space; and the bold geometry of the pattern that she presents—especially the black vertical bar at the base of her coronet, and the directed curves at the back of her gown—strengthens the vector of her outstretched arm. But Alice is not moved. She stands her ground with arms crossed in a comfortably self-protective posture, insulated from disturbances by an umbral halo (all the other characters have to compete against a cluttered background to be seen at all), her head cocked just enough to look her accuser defiantly in the eye. She virtually ignores the accusing finger.

Aside from being the only character to stand out clearly against the background, Alice is the character closest to the picture plane, and the only character entirely modeled in three dimensions. The farther back from the picture plane (and the farther back from Alice), the flatter the character: this is an ordinary effect of perspective, which Tenniel has pointedly exaggerated. The Queen, almost as far forward as Alice, has a fully modeled face and arm, and her foot protrudes forward convincingly; but the rest of her is all one plane, as flat as the playing card she derives from. The Knave has somewhat less three-dimensional reality than the Queen, and a good deal less than the pillow that he holds in his hands. The King's left arm and scepter cast shadows on

Fig. 6.1. Tenniel. Alice and the Queen of Hearts. From *Alice's Adventures in Wonderland*.

his robe; that is the only detail that saves him from being a mere pasteboard figure, like the other court cards to be glimpsed farther back. Behind those stand ranks of faceless cards, whose flatness, parallel to the picture plane, is reinforced by the flat planes of the topiary hedges behind them.

And yet those hedges are obviously thick and rounded, at least as three-dimensional as the fountain that plays in front of them. And behind the hedges, masses of trees imply considerable depth, as do the birds in the air; and hovering in the midst of the background is the sizable spaciousness of the glass conservatory. So the perspectival flattening that controls the social foreground of Tenniel's picture does not control the horticultural background, where, on the contrary, things resume a fully-dimensioned reality.

Clearly Alice, the exceptional figure in the foreground, belongs more to the world of the garden (where indeed she has wanted to go since chapter 1) than to the world of the social figures who are blocking her path and walling her out.

The hierarchy of reality according to which Tenniel ranks the figures in the foreground corresponds to the degrees of complexity that the figures present in Carroll's story in general, or at this particular point in the story. Alice is the only character in the book who might be called a "round" character in E. M. Forster's sense; that is, one who is "capable of surprising in a convincing way."[2] The Queen is relatively inflexible and predictable; like the Mrs. Micawber of Forster's example, she can easily be summarized in a phrase; and yet she has a certain capacity to surprise, at least on this first encounter, and so gets a degree of modeling. The Knave is even more completely defined by his simple knavish role in the history of the tarts. What complexity he has he gets not from Carroll but from Tenniel, who allows him a rounded countenance (here as in the frontispiece, figure 3.1) suggestive of a smug satisfaction in his knavery. The King at this point of the story is the least independent of all the principal characters, useful to swell the Queen's progress, and little else. (He becomes a more rounded character when he presides at the trial in chapter 12; see figure 3.4). Aside from Alice the only fully rounded character to be seen in this garden is the White Rabbit, who stands almost invisible behind the Knave, well out of his hierarchical place and almost out of the picture. What he is doing there at all is hard to say. (That may indeed be the point, if what he represents is the surplus of the signifier.)[3]

Tenniel's assigning to the characters in this illustration various degrees of solidity is an elegant solution to a problem that evidently daunted Carroll when he illustrated the story himself, in the gift manuscript for Alice Liddell. Figure 6.2 is Carroll's drawing of the end of the royal procession to the

Fig. 6.2. Carroll. Royal procession to the garden. From *Alice's Adventures under Ground*.

garden; it can be seen here, as in other illustrations in the manuscript, that he had trouble reconciling the two-dimensional patterning of the costumes of standard nineteenth-century court cards with the three-dimensional quality that those cards as characters would have in Alice's dream. (Figure 6.3 shows a representative actual card, a knave of hearts printed in England in 1832.)[4] But Tenniel, a professional artist, could interpret figure and pattern in any degree of three-dimensionality that he chose. In the frontispiece to *Alice's Adventures* (fig. 3.1), the body of the Knave of Hearts is as flat as it is in the garden scene, but the Queen and her formally patterned gown are both presented in a conventionally modeled, foreshortened three-dimensionality.

Carroll's illustration of the procession is an obvious prototype for Tenniel's garden illustration. From it Tenniel got,

Fig. 6.3. Thomas de la Rue. Knave of hearts playing card. Museo de Naipes, Vitoria, Spain; reproduced by courtesy of F. A. Fournier.

besides the principal characters, some details that are not specified at this point in the text: the fountain (although fountains were included in Alice's first glimpse of the garden, in chapter 1), the low fencing, the enlarged crown, and the reduction of the gardeners to ordinary playing cards. For the parasol that Carroll put in the Queen's hand Tenniel substituted a fan, because he could render it emblematically heart-shaped. Otherwise, nothing in Carroll's original picture has been left out.

A great deal has been added, however, and from several sources. Alice and the Queen do not confront each other in Carroll's drawing of the procession, but they do in his last illustration to the story proper, when Alice rejects as "nonsense" the Queen's idea of courtroom procedure ("first the sentence, and then the evidence"). Figure 6.4 shows the Queen responding angrily to this rejection: " 'Hold your tongue!' said the Queen. 'I won't!' said Alice, 'you're nothing but a pack of cards! Who cares for you?' "

This is a highly charged moment in the story, indeed so highly charged that it fast brings the dream to an end. The fact that it turns on Alice's rejection of the Queen's discourse as "nonsense" allies it with the moment in the garden that occurs just after the moment illustrated in figure 6.1, when Alice rejects the Queen's order of execution. " 'Nonsense!' said Alice, very loudly and decidedly, and the Queen was silent." These two moments of rejection by Alice are structurally the same, which explains why Tenniel incorporated Carroll's visualization of the final scene into his representation of the quarrel in the garden.

Certain aspects of figure 6.4 have already been noticed in figure 6.1: the fact that the Queen admonishes Alice from a superior height, and the fact that Alice cocks her head up to face down the Queen's anger. And though Tenniel has turned the Queen to show her in profile, it is obvious that his rendition of Alice's impassive head (the more impassive because her expression is not shown) is modeled closely on Carroll's.

Certain other details Tenniel drew not from Carroll's example but from his own experience as a staff cartoonist for *Punch*. The topiary arched hedges in the garden, for example, derive from the Fragonardesque garden scene that Tenniel provided the British royal family in *Punch's Pocket Book for 1857* (fig. 6.5), directly above a listing of their birth

"Now for the evidence," said the King, "and then the sentence.

"No!" said the Queen, first the sentence, and then the evidence!"

"Nonsense!" cried Alice, so loudly that everybody jumped, the idea of having the sentence first!

"Hold your tongue!" said the Queen.

"I won't!" said Alice, "you're nothing but a pack of cards! Who cares for you?"

Fig. 6.4. Carroll. Alice and the Queen of Hearts. From *Alice's Adventures under Ground.*

dates. This scene is the contrary of the garden scene in *Alice's Adventures*. The Queen (Victoria) here looks benignly on the pastime of her daughter (Mary Louisa, the Princess Royal), who amuses herself by making a pet of the ferocious British lion (compare figure 1.44). All terror is here sublimated in play; even the stolen bird's nest, a dreaded loss in chapter 5 ("You're looking for eggs, I know *that* well enough," the Pigeon tells Alice), makes a pleasant gift for a little girl in this pastoral landscape.

The connection between these two scenes is secured by the detail of the crown which surmounts the lower border of figure 6.5. It is the same crown, *mutatis mutandis*, that the Knave of Hearts carries on his pillow: St. Edward's crown, the state crown of England, complete with fleurs-de-lys and quadruple arches. The cross that tops St. Edward's crown is hard to make out in figure 6.5; in figure 6.1 it is replaced by a more fitting heart. (A minor cross at the base of the central arch is missing from both versions.) From the early eighteenth century on, a representation of St. Edward's crown appeared on every ace of spades printed in England, to certify payment of a special duty on playing cards. Figure 6.6 shows a late eighteenth-century example, in which the artist has made the arches about as angular as Tenniel does. Figure 6.7 shows an early Victorian version of the crown, part of a bookseller's royal warrant. In nineteenth-century England

THE STATE.

THE ROYAL FAMILY OF ENGLAND.

	Born
QUEEN ALEXANDRINA VICTORIA (Acc. June 20, 1837) .	May 24, 1819
Prince Albert Francis Augustus Charles Emanuel . .	Aug. 26, 1819
Albert Edward, Prince of Wales	Nov. 9, 1841
Albert Ernest Alfred	Aug. 6, 1844

Fig. 6.5. Tenniel. "The Royal Family of England." From *Punch's Pocket Book for 1857.* The Beinecke Rare Book and Manuscript Library, Yale University.

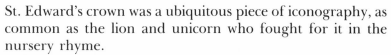

Fig. 6.6. J. Hardy. Ace of spades playing card. By permission of the Worshipful Company of Makers of Playing Cards, London.

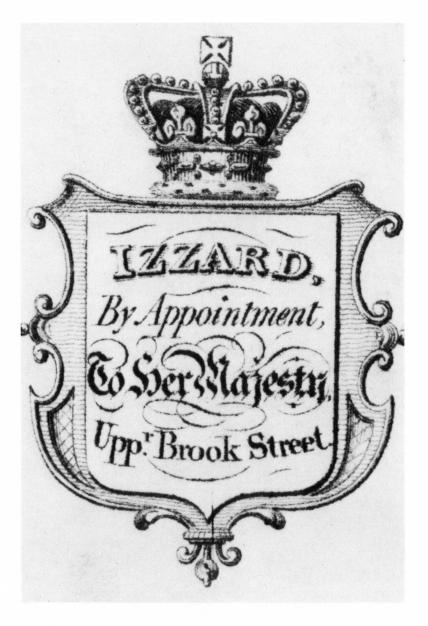

Fig. 6.7. Bookseller's royal warrant, showing St. Edward's crown. Private collection.

St. Edward's crown was a ubiquitous piece of iconography, as common as the lion and unicorn who fought for it in the nursery rhyme.

Tenniel's incorporation of St. Edward's crown into Alice's fantasy would have made that fantasy a familiar one for any Victorian child reader. It has sometimes been suggested that the Queen of Hearts looks a bit like Queen Victoria; and Tenniel's drawing of Victoria in figure 6.5 provides a sketchy ground for comparison. The three-quarters profile of the Queen of Hearts in figure 6.8 compares more directly to that of Queen Victoria in figure 6.9 (*Punch*, 23 September 1865). Tenniel drew this cartoon the same year as the *Alice* illustrations, as part of a general campaign to bring the widowed queen back into public life. The Queen of Hearts is older and uglier than this obviously idealized figure, but there is a clear resemblance.

Carroll, a fervent admirer of Queen Victoria, once pretended that she had invited him to one of her garden parties; figure 6.10 shows the handwritten invitation from Victoria that he forged for the entertainment of some child friends.[5] But despite occasional contact with members of the royal family, Carroll was never honored with any real invitation of this sort, and Alice's audience in Tenniel's garden is as close as he ever came to conversing with his Queen.

Aside from the Queen herself, the most imposing Victorian motif in figure 6.1 is the hemispherical glass conservatory looming in the background, an unprecedented triumph of nineteenth-century engineering. Greenhouse architecture had culminated in the spectacular Crystal Palace

QUEEN HERMIONE.

Paulina (Britannia) Unveils the Statue. "'TIS TIME! DESCEND; BE STONE NO MORE!"

Winter's Tale, Act V., Scene 3.

Fig. 6.9. Tenniel. "Queen Hermione" (Queen Victoria). From *Punch*, 23 September 1865.

Fig. 6.8. Tenniel. The Queen of Hearts in conference. From *Alice's Adventures in Wonderland*.

of 1851, which Tenniel illustrated for *Punch* as an epitome of British progress (figs. 6.11 and 6.12).[6] So far as I know, purely hemispherical greenhouses like that shown in figure 6.1 were never attempted. The Anthaeum (or Antheum) at Hove was planned by Henry Phillips to be an immense unsupported glass dome, but more than twice as broad as tall, and topped off with a cupola (figure 6.13 is a projected rendering); and it collapsed before completion in the summer of 1833. The same architect had recently completed a more modest squat dome, which for many years was a popular attraction at the Surrey Zoological Gardens (fig. 6.14).[7]

A careful reader of *Punch* might have recognized in Tenniel's Queen of Hearts the identity of another queen than Queen Victoria, a kind of anti-Victoria, a queen notorious for her "frailty": Queen Gertrude, the wife of Claudius and mother of Hamlet. Gertrude dominates one of the two "Illustrations to Shakespeare" that satirize *Hamlet*. It takes its text from the closet scene, as Hamlet eulogizes his father, King Hamlet, for having possessed:

> Hyperion's curls, the front of Jove himself,
> An eye like Mars, to threaten and command,
> A station like the herald Mercury
> New lighted on a heaven-kissing hill—
> A combination and a form indeed
> Where every god did seem to set his seal
> To give the world assurance of a man.
>   [III.iv.57–63.]

Taking the second of these lines for a caption and punning from "Mars" to "Ma's," Tenniel drew the curiously familiar scene of figure 6.15 (*Punch*, 22 September 1855), in which Queen Gertrude threatens and commands quite in the attitude of the Queen of Hearts, if with more emphasis upon her evil eye and less upon shouting. By transferring the royal prerogatives of threat and command from King Hamlet to his wife Queen Gertrude, and by reducing them in the process to the arbitrary bluster of a querulous middle-aged woman, the *Punch* editors and Tenniel foreshadowed the decay of the authority of the King of Hearts into the petty willfulness of his Queen. Furthermore, Tenniel's cartoon on the closet scene, in which Hamlet decried his mother's sensuality, corroborates what many readers have suspected: that the threat which the Queen of Hearts presents to Alice is chiefly maternal and sexual.

Another ominous element of this Queen's identity would have been available not only to readers of *Punch* but to anyone who had ever played with an early nineteenth-century set of playing cards. Tenniel's image of the King of Hearts is taken directly from the standard playing card pattern (fig. 6.16); this adoption is most obvious in figure 6.1. We have

already seen that Tenniel's Knave of Hearts conforms to this pattern. But Tenniel obviously did not draw his Queen of Hearts after the usual prototype (fig. 6.17). (For one thing, the bold checkered collar of the playing card is missing from figure 6.1; instead a scarf crosses in front of the bodice.) Nor is Tenniel's Queen of Hearts dressed like any Queen in nineteenth-century illustrations to the nursery rhyme (for example, figures 6.18, 6.19, 6.20, 6.21).[8] Instead, Tenniel has dressed her in the clothes of her playing-card rival and nemesis, the queen of spades, the queen of death (fig. 6.22).

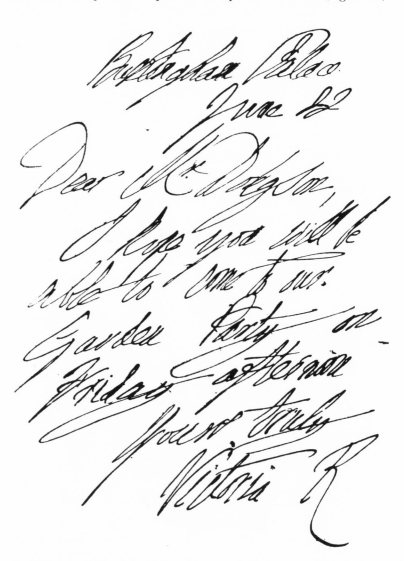

Fig. 6.10. Carroll. Fabricated invitation from Queen Victoria. From Derek Hudson, *Lewis Carroll* (1954); reprinted by permission of Constable & Company Ltd.

It may be that Tenniel preferred the robes of the queen of spades for purely formal reasons, so as to incorporate the triangular back panel of her gown, with its array of arrows, into the sweeping vectors that he focused onto the Queen's pointing finger. Or it may be that he dressed Carroll's Queen of Hearts like the queen of spades because the quality that she brings to Alice's nightmare is not love but the fear of death.[9] If Tenniel's gesture was not merely formal but serious, Alice's response to the Queen's savage command, "Off with her head! Off—", is the more eloquently effective. "'Nonsense!' said Alice, very loudly and decidedly, and the Queen was silent."

Fig. 6.11. Tenniel. "The Modern Aesop," showing the Crystal Palace. From *Punch*, January–June 1851.

THE HAPPY FAMILY IN HYDE PARK.

Fig. 6.12. Tenniel. "The Happy Family in Hyde Park," showing the Crystal Palace. From *Punch*, July–December 1851.

Fig. 6.13. The Anthaeum at Hove. Reprinted by permission of the Brighton Reference Library, East Sussex.

Fig. 6.14. Dome at Surrey Zoological Gardens. From *Gardener's Magazine*, December (1831).

123

Fig. 6.15. Tenniel. "An eye like MARS." From *Punch*, 22 September 1855.

Fig. 6.17. Thomas de la Rue. Queen of hearts playing card. From Museo de Naipes, Vitoria, Spain; reproduced by courtesy of F. A. Fournier.

Fig. 6.16. Thomas de la Rue. King of hearts playing card. From Museo de Naipes, Vitoria, Spain; reproduced by courtesy of F. A. Fournier.

Fig. 6.18. William Mulready. "The King of Hearts." From *The King and Queen of Hearts* (1806); rpt. *The Works of Charles and Mary Lamb* (1903).

Fig. 6.19. William Mulready. "And vow'd he'd steal no more." From *The King and Queen of Hearts* (1806); rpt. *The Works of Charles and Mary Lamb* (1903).

Fig. 6.20. King, Queen, and Knave of Hearts. From *Songs for the Nursery* (1851); reproduced by Iona and Peter Opie, eds., *The Oxford Nursery Rhyme Book* (1955; rpt. 1977). Reprinted by permission of Clarendon Press, Oxford University Press.

Fig. 6.22. Thomas de la Rue. Queen of spades playing card. From Museo de Naipes, Vitoria, Spain; reproduced by courtesy of F. A. Fournier.

Fig. 6.21. Percy Cruikshank. King, Queen, and Knave of Hearts. From *The Queen of Hearts Alphabet* (c. 1865); reproduced by Iona and Peter Opie, eds., *Three Centuries of Nursery Rhymes and Poetry for Children* (1973). Reprinted by permission of Iona Opie.

CHAPTER SEVEN

The Invention of the White Knight

In *The History of "Punch"* (1895), M. H. Spielmann incidentally publicized a belief that John Tenniel's drawings of the White Knight in Lewis Carroll's *Through the Looking-Glass* (figs. 7.1, 7.2, and 7.3, drawn about

Fig. 7.2. Tenniel. The White Knight and the aged man. From *Through the Looking-Glass.*

Fig. 7.1. Tenniel. The White Knight and Alice. Frontispiece to *Through the Looking-Glass.*

Fig. 7.3. Tenniel. The White Knight and Alice. From *Through the Looking-Glass.*

1870) were also caricatures of Tenniel's friend and colleague, Horace "Ponny" Mayhew.[1] Presumably this belief had been held by some members of the *Punch* staff. Since the mid sixties, Tenniel had been the chief cartoonist at *Punch*; and Horace Mayhew, younger brother of the cofounder Henry Mayhew, was a well-liked factotum on the staff.

Even as he publicized this notion, Spielmann took pains to discredit it. He quoted a denial that Tenniel had made, probably in a letter written to Spielmann in the early nineties, responding to enquiries. This is Spielmann's whole account:

> "Ponny's" portrait, it has often been said, may be seen in the White Knight in "Alice in Wonderland" [a casual reference to the sequel, *Through the Looking-Glass*]; but "the resemblance," says Sir John Tenniel, "was purely accidental, a mere unintentional caricature, which his *friends*, of course, were only too delighted to make the most of. P. M. was certainly handsome, whereas the White Knight can scarcely be considered a type of 'manly beauty.' "[2]

Spielmann does say that Mayhew "was a strikingly good-looking man." Evidently, too, he was a bon vivant and man-about-town, unlike Carroll's Knight. But there are a few obvious points of comparison: both men were a little slow-witted; both were bachelors; both were mostly bald.[3]

Some readers of Spielmann's *History* have taken Tenniel's disclaimer into account. In his memoirs Harry Furniss, who followed Tenniel both on the staff of *Punch* and as an illustrator for Lewis Carroll (*Sylvie and Bruno*), quoted Tenniel's reply as definitive. And in her monograph on Tenniel, Frances Sarzano mentioned both the theory and the denial. But the two historians of *Punch* who wrote after Spielmann are more casual about the matter. R. G. G. Price offers the unqualified report that Tenniel sketched a "picture of his colleague Ponny Mayhew as Carroll's White Knight." And Arthur Prager writes that Mayhew's "friend and drinking companion John Tenniel used Ponny as his model for the White Knight in Lewis Carroll's *Through the Looking-Glass*. Today Ponny Mayhew is probably the only Punchite whose features would be instantly recognizable to literate people."[4]

Given these two conflicting traditions, both derived from Spielmann's book, one wonders what Ponny Mayhew actually looked like, why the *Punch* staffers assumed that Tenniel's White Knight caricatured him, and whether Tenniel's denial, made some twenty years after the fact, is plausible.

Spielmann's *History* itself provides enough evidence to judge these questions. It includes a small photograph of Mayhew, taken at an uncertain date (fig. 7.4), and also two caricature sketches by Tenniel's predecessors on the *Punch*

Fig. 7.4. Bassano. Photograph of Horace Mayhew. From M. H. Spielmann, *The History of "Punch"* (1895).

art staff, John Leech and Richard Doyle. Figure 7.5 is a detail from an 1847 Leech cartoon that represents the *Punch* staff as a musical band; according to Spielmann (pp. 261–62), the cornetist at the extreme left is Mayhew. Figure 7.6 is a sketch by Richard Doyle, probably drawn before 1850 (when he left the magazine); Spielmann credits Mayhew with the minimal profile on the extreme right (p. 337). It is obvious from these two caricatures, if not from the tiny photograph, that Mayhew had a pronounced, hooked nose, rather like that of the

Fig. 7.5. John Leech. *Punch* staff as musical band (cartoon detail). From
M. H. Spielmann, *The History of "Punch"* (1895).

Fig. 7.6. Richard Doyle. Sketch of John
Leech, Tom Taylor, and Horace Mayhew. From M. H. Spielmann, *The History
of "Punch"* (1895).

White Knight, which is displayed prominently in Tenniel's
frontispiece (fig. 7.1). But the Leech cartoon shows a relatively young Mayhew, and the Doyle caricature is less than
sketchy. Altogether, the evidence of these three images is
inconclusive.

The matter is not settled even by a caricature of Mayhew
that Tenniel drew himself, in 1854 (fig. 7.7).[5] Mayhew is
playing leapfrog just to the right of center. (The other *Punch*
staffers shown here include the artist, who is decorating a
wall with a graffito of Mr. Punch—who is, as often in *Punch*, a
knight at arms himself.) Here Mayhew does look as the
White Knight conceivably might have looked in his younger
days. But again the age difference counts against any definite
identification.

Fortunately, Spielmann's book includes one more relevant
image, which seems to be decisive. Late in 1869 or early in
1870 George du Maurier, Tenniel's junior colleague on the
art staff, drew a caricature of Mayhew that confirms, and
indeed may have inspired, the old supposition that the White
Knight bears more than an accidental resemblance to Mayhew. This caricature was part of a printed invitation form
sent out each week to summon *Punch* staff members to their
elaborate dinner meetings, at which much of the week-to-
week planning was done (fig. 7.8). According to Spielmann
(p. 69) the winged head responding to the call on the right
represents Tenniel, who was of course a regular guest at
these dinners; and that in the center is Mayhew, another
regular guest (with du Maurier himself in tow). In almost all
its details, this profile caricature of Ponny Mayhew closely
matches Tenniel's frontispiece profile of the White Knight
(fig. 7.1.). No wonder the *Punch* staff saw Mayhew in the
Looking-Glass antihero.

Fig. 7.7. Tenniel. The *Punch* staff at play. From *Punch*, July–December 1854.

Fig. 7.8. George du Maurier. *Punch* dinner invitation card. From M. H. Spielmann, *The History of "Punch"* (1895).

As for Tenniel's disclaimer, there is the broadly discrediting fact that two decades had passed between the *Looking-Glass* drawings and his reply to Spielmann. His specific objection that Mayhew was too handsome may have been based on old memories of Mayhew in his youth. And, as Tenniel almost hints himself, he need not have caricatured Mayhew consciously and directly. He may have unconsciously assimilated du Maurier's profile sketch of him, which, because of its context, he would have seen dozens of times, week after week, during the very months when he was preparing the *Looking-Glass* illustrations.[6]

Tenniel took pride in the fact that he usually drew the visual imagery of his cartoons from the visual imagery in his head, hardly ever having to resort to the direct study of objects or models of any sort. But what made this possible, as he once remarked to Spielmann, was that "anything I see I

Fig. 7.9. Photograph of John Tenniel. By permission of the British Museum.

Fig. 7.10. Tenniel. Self-portrait. From M. H. Spielmann, *The History of "Punch"* (1895).

remember."[7] He certainly saw du Maurier's sketch of Mayhew, and in some sense "remembered" it when he sat down to illustrate chapter 8 of *Through the Looking-Glass*.

Carroll strongly objected to the image of the White Knight that resulted. "The White Knight must not have whiskers; he must not be made to look old," he insisted in a letter—but to no effect.[8] To overcome such objections Tenniel must have had more than a casual commitment to what he had drawn.

Aside from Mayhew the only other person thought to be a possible prototype for Tenniel's White Knight is Tenniel himself. John Pudney, citing an apparently undated portrait photograph now in the British Museum (fig. 7.9), has commented that "the features of the White Knight bear a remarkable resemblance to the illustrator's own."[9] That photograph looks to be contemporary with a pen-and-ink self-portrait that Tenniel dated "1889" (fig. 7.10).[10] If so, the resemblance that Pudney sees is a matter of life imitating art. Two decades earlier, at the time Tenniel was actually drawing the White Knight, he probably resembled his subject less closely. Indeed, on the evidence of du Maurier's contemporary sketch (fig. 7.8), Tenniel then still had a distinct thatch of hair, and all in all resembled the White Knight far less than Mayhew then did.

This is too bad, for Pudney's suggestion is very appealing. We know that Carroll's White Knight is something of an autobiographical satire; it would be fitting if Tenniel's White Knight were too.

But art isn't always that pat. Prager seems closer to the truth than Pudney. Ponny Mayhew, and not John Tenniel, "is probably the only Punchite whose features"—although mediated by du Maurier's pen—"would be instantly recognizable to literate people."

CHAPTER EIGHT

The Descent of the Jabberwock

The day after Christmas in 1868, *Punch* published a nightmarish vision drawn by Tenniel's friend and colleague on the art staff, George du Maurier. This cartoon, titled "A Little Christmas Dream" (fig. 8.1), is in several respects a prototype for Tenniel's famous *Looking-Glass* illustration of a young knight confronting the Jabberwock (fig. 8.2). As striking as the sameness of the subject-matter—a boy menaced by a monster—is the basic similarity of the organization of these two pictures, with the boy in each one placed in a foreground corner, looking diagonally across towards the monster farther back, who almost fills the opposite half of the picture. Though the different monsters descend from different stock (du Maurier's is mainly a mammoth, Tenniel's mainly a dragon), they carry their tusks, claws, and heads in the same menacing configuration (secondary head, in the du Maurier). The city street and the path in the woods too are much the same, with the houses, lamp posts, and picket fence of the one replaced by the thicket of trees of the other.

Originally planned as the frontispiece to *Through the Looking-Glass*, Tenniel's drawing was relegated to the middle of chapter 1 when Lewis Carroll decided, after having consulted the mothers of representative potential readers, that it was indeed (as had been suggested to him) "too terrible a monster, and likely to alarm nervous and imaginative children."[1]

Of course nervous and imaginative children would be terrified as much by the weakness of the protagonist as by the power of the monster. They would identify with Tenniel's seemingly frail, childlike knight—"Childe," in the nomenclature of the old ballads, which the poem "Jabberwocky" parodies. This child knight seems the androgynous projection of Alice's own fears: he closely resembles the Alice of figure 8.3, leaning back with long hair hanging down. (In that picture, having mastered the monstrous poem "Jabberwocky" by interpreting it for Alice, Humpty Dumpty has taken the monster's place.) Neither Alice nor her chivalric counterpart looks strong enough for self defense. As Alexander L. Taylor has commented, Tenniel's little hero "could not possibly galumph," let alone slay dragons.[2]

In its way the du Maurier picture is even more alarming. The terror of the Jabberwock is at least partly undercut by its myopic expression and middle-class waistcoat and spats, but the terror of the du Maurier monster is unmitigated. The doubled heads and gaping mouth are obviously threatening; more subtle is the carelessness of the extra figure of the policeman, who twirls his baton as he patrols the street, unseeing. The snow freezing to the boy's feet realizes the anxious dream motif of arrested flight that Freud would soon study in *The Interpretation of Dreams* (1900). It does not take much analysis to recognize the unknowing bobby as a neglectful father figure—the antitype of the supportive father to whom Carroll's hero will report his surprising victory over the Jabberwock. In du Maurier's nightmare such a happy ending is unimaginable.

Like the Tenniel drawing, the du Maurier cartoon is a kind of book illustration, but displaced. It is a satiric comment on *The World before the Deluge* by Louis Figuier, a book of popular paleontology that had achieved five editions in the original French and two editions (1865, 1866) in English translation. The cartoon's caption is largely self-explanatory:

Mr. L. Figuier, in the Thesis which precedes his interesting work on the world before the Flood, condemns the practice of awakening the youthful mind to admiration by means of fables and fairy tales, and recommends, in lieu thereof, the study of the natural history of the world in which we live. Fired by this advice, we have tried the experiment on our eldest, an imaginative boy of six. We have cut off his "Cinderella" and his "Puss in Boots," and introduced him to some of the more peaceful fauna of the preadamite world, as they appear restored in Mr. Figuier's book.

The poor boy has not had a decent night's rest ever since!

A LITTLE CHRISTMAS DREAM.

Although Figuier writes as if his proposals were new, they are in the tradition of Rousseau's *Émile* (1762).[3] Figuier wants to deny children fables, fairy tales, myths, and all such "purely imaginative" readings, because such stories condition "weak and irresolute minds, given to credulity, inclined to mysticism—proselytes, in advance, to chimerical conceptions and to every extravagant system." He acknowledges that "the

Fig. 8.3. Tenniel. Alice and Humpty Dumpty. From *Through the Looking-Glass*.

Fig. 8.1 (opposite). George du Maurier. "A Little Christmas Dream." From *Punch*, 26 December 1868.

Fig. 8.2. Tenniel. The Jabberwock and the young knight. From *Through the Looking-Glass*.

imaginative faculty, which permits of ideality and of the abstract,—which forms poets, inventors, and artists,—is inherent in the mind, and cannot be suppressed; it can only perish with it. It is the integral part of intelligence." But he maintains that that faculty can best be exercised on the things of this world, in "the study of nature." The works of the Creator are marvelous enough for any childish or adult imagination, and their study both educates the reasoning faculty and leads to a proper reverence for the Creator. Even geology, if properly understood, will strengthen piety; and it has the advantage over fairy tales that it is scientifically true, and good for the mind.

What Figuier seems not to notice, but what du Maurier seizes upon as the basis for his cartoon, is the fact that this essay in "science" carries with it a large number of fantastic woodcut illustrations, not factual and pietistic but imaginative and profane. A conjectured monster is no less fabulous for having a scientific name, and several of the illustrations in *The World before the Deluge* could do just what Figuier feared, that is, "cultivate and excite that inclination for the marvellous which is already excessive in the human mind."

Fig. 8.4. Édouard Riou. "Skeleton of the Mammoth in the St. Petersburg Museum." From Louis Figuier, *The World before the Deluge* (1865; rpt. 1866).

Fig. 8.5. Édouard Riou. "Mammoth restored." From Louis Figuier, *The World before the Deluge* (1865; rpt. 1866).

Not that there is anything very extravagant about the illustrations of the mammoth skeleton and reconstructed mammoth in Figuier's book, which are the immediate prototypes for du Maurier's monster (figs. 8.4, 8.5). But these illustrations were not part of the main series of illustrations by the artist Édouard Riou, called "ideal landscapes" or "ideal scenes," which together made up the chief interest of the book. These pictures included visions of some remarkably sublime monsters: for example, figures 8.6 and 8.7. Instead of becoming extinct, these monsters had progeny that still flourish in sensational (and profitable) "dinosaur books" for children. Appropriately, Riou's high-Romantic penchant for the fabulous side of science later made him an authorized illustrator of the scientific fantasies of Jules Verne.[4]

The haberdashery that Tenniel used to humanize the Jabberwock recalls the outfits of several dragons that he had drawn for *Punch* early in his career, all ornamental initials

Fig. 8.6. Édouard Riou. "Ideal scene of the Lias with Ichthyosaurus and Plesiosaurus." From Louis Figuier, *The World before the Deluge* (1865; rpt. 1866).

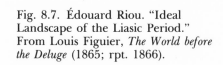

Fig. 8.7. Édouard Riou. "Ideal Landscape of the Liasic Period." From Louis Figuier, *The World before the Deluge* (1865; rpt. 1866).

Fig. 8.8. Tenniel. Ornamental initial. From *Punch*, January–June 1851.

Fig. 8.9. Tenniel. Ornamental initial. From *Punch*, July–December 1852.

Fig. 8.10. Tenniel. Ornamental initial. From *Punch*, July–December 1853.

(figs. 8.8, 8.9, 8.10). Figure 8.9 varies the stock *Punch* theme of St. George and the dragon (figs. 8.11, 8.12, 8.13).[5] The culmination of this motif was the title page that Tenniel drew for volume 37 (1859), in which Mr. Punch, armed not as a medieval but as a Greek warrior, triumphs over the monster of "cant," "folly," and "humbug" (fig. 8.14). When this image is held upside down in front of a mirror, the kinship between the dragon and the *Looking-Glass* Jabberwock becomes more obvious, especially in the wings and the trailing tail. And of course Mr. Punch's hobbyhorse will also reappear in *Looking-Glass*, not much metamorphosed, as the Rocking-horse-fly. (fig. 8.15). Hobbyhorses in this style, as drawn by John Leech and others as well as by Tenniel, were standard props in *Punch*; figure 8.14 is only the most striking example.

In addition to the du Maurier and Tenniel cartoons that prefigure the Jabberwock, there is also an Old Master painting. Francis Huxley recently drew attention to an engraving after a painting by Salvator Rosa, which had been printed in William Hone's *Every-Day Book and Table Book*—an early Victorian calendar, elaborately annotated and illustrated, which was often reprinted. Carroll himself owned a copy.[6] The entry for 17 January is devoted to the life of St. Anthony, the patron saint of monks, whose religious retreat had been tested repeatedly by devils in many guises, including that of an exceptionally hideous monster. The engraving by Samuel Williams with which Hone illustrates this hagiography (fig. 8.16) is a simplified rendering of Rosa's *The Temptation of St. Anthony*, long in the Pitti Palace in Florence (fig. 8.17). The perspective of this engraving does indeed anticipate that of the Jabberwock; the monsters have several features in common; and the old saint's cross and young knight's sword are functionally as well as visually equivalent.

Whether or not Tenniel knew this particular engraving or the painting on which it is based, he certainly knew the topic that they illustrate. One of his first large drawings for *Punch*, an illustration to an anticlerical travesty called "The Saints of Old," shows (in the upper left-hand corner) St. Anthony, asleep, being menaced by an ineffectual dragon as loutish as

Fig. 8.11. Tenniel. St. George and the dragon. From *Punch*, July–December 1851.

Fig. 8.12. Tenniel. St. George and the dragon. From *Punch*, July–December 1851.

Fig. 8.13. Tenniel. St. George and the dragon. From *Punch*, January–June 1852.

the Jabberwock (fig. 8.18). Two stanzas in the *Punch* ballad motivate this vignette and also the one opposite:

> Talk of Jumpers, talk of Shakers, and their antics
>   queer and quaint!
> They are all nothing; none but Fakirs can approach
>   your ancient Saint.
> Thus he lived without a neighbour, or a soul to love
>   or please,
> Working not, and giving labour only to industrious
>   fleas.
>   Sing the cock-bird is the gander, and the goose
>   the gander's hen;
>   And these, my bucks, were your holy men!
>
> Now he lay in trances snoring—now his occupation dull
> Was to sit intently poring on an image or a skull;
> With these employments interfered the Fiend, with imps
>   in various shapes,
> Who, to annoy the Saint, appeared as dragons, owls,
>   wild beasts, and apes.
>   Sing, &c.[7]

Just as likely as the Williams engraving to have caught Tenniel's attention is the engraving of the same painting, by F. W. Fairholt, in Thomas Wright's *A History of Caricature and Grotesque* (fig. 8.19). Despite the shadows of the forest, Tenniel's monster is a brighter and firmer image than Williams'; it has more in common with Fairholt's more analytic "outline" version.[8]

It happens that Lewis Carroll's later advisor on artistic matters, John Ruskin, had strongly mixed emotions about Salvator Rosa. He feared, and condemned as meretricious, Salvator's penchant for the terrible and the Sublime: "The base and vicious painters, of whom Salvator stands far ahead the basest—unapproachably and inexpressibly detestable—a very abyss of abomination—these as a class—and Salvator chiefly as representative of them, are attracted by terror—and skilful in arousing it in others." But Salvator's *St. Anthony*, which Ruskin studied in the Pitti Palace, had a great appeal for him; he thought that in it "such power as the artist possessed is fully manifested, and less offensively than is usual in his sacred subjects." The painting showed Salvator to be "capable of fear"—fear of damnation. In the following

Fig. 8.14 (opposite). Tenniel. Mr. Punch as a Greek warrior. From *Punch*, July–December 1859.

Fig. 8.15. Tenniel. Rocking-horse-fly. From *Through the Looking-Glass*.

account, Salvator seems to merge with St. Anthony himself—who also shares the perspective of the onlooker and art critic: "The gray spectre, horse-headed, striding across the sky . . . its bat wings spread, green bars of the twilight seen between its bones; it was no play to him—the painting of it. Helpless Salvator! A little early sympathy, a word of true guidance, perhaps, had saved him."[9]

Ruskin's responses to this picture are worth considering here as a substitute for what Carroll's own responses would have been, had he seen the painting. Collegiate monastics at Christ Church, Ruskin and Carroll suffered many of the same temptations (including affection for Alice Liddell), and much the same sense of guilt. Ruskin's guilt eventually gave way to madness; Carroll evaded his by constructing intellectual puzzles in the sleepless hours of night, to ward off the torment of evil thoughts. It could as well be said of each of them what the art historian Carl Linfert has said of St. Anthony, whom Bosch and many others besides Salvator painted in his distress: "What attracted Bosch was the true content of this man's life: the resistance he put up to onslaughts against his virtue which, admittedly, came mostly as visions, so that the saint scarcely had much occasion to become familiar with the real world, the flesh, and real devils."[10]

When he relegated Tenniel's monstrous frontispiece to the inside of his book, Carroll was protecting himself as well as "nervous and impressionable children." The mock-heroic note that Tenniel struck was not strong enough a defense. Because of its descent from Salvator's sublime demon—the tormentor of an ascetic saint—Tenniel's Jabberwock was indeed "too terrible a monster."

Fig. 8.16. Samuel Williams, after Salvator Rosa. *The Temptation of St. Anthony.* From William Hone, *Every-Day Book and Table Book* (n.d.)

Fig. 8.17. Salvator Rosa. *The Temptation of St. Anthony.* Painting. The Pitti Palace, Florence. Alinari / Art Resource, Inc.

Fig. 8.18. Tenniel. "The Saints of Old." From *Punch*, January–June 1851.

Fig. 8.19. F. W. Fairholt, after Salvator Rosa. *The Temptation of St. Anthony.* From Thomas Wright, *A History of Caricature & the Grotesque in Literature and Art* (1865).

CHAPTER NINE

"Looking-Glass Insects"

The most commonly cited link between *Punch* and *Alice* is the supposed presence in *Through the Looking-Glass* of two stock characters from Tenniel's political cartoons, Benjamin Disraeli and William Ewart Gladstone. Chapter 3, "Looking-Glass Insects," includes Tenniel's illustration of Alice in a railway compartment; by an established convention the man across from her, wearing a paper hat and otherwise "dressed in white paper," is Benjamin Disraeli (fig. 9.1). This idea may belong to William Empson, who introduced it casually in his influential study of the *Alice* books, a chapter in *Some Versions of Pastoral* (1935):

> In the *Looking-Glass* too there are ideas about progress at an early stage of the journey of growing up. Alice goes quickly through the first square by railway, in a carriage full of animals in a state of excitement about the progress of business and machinery; the only man is Disraeli dressed in newspapers—the new man who gets on by self-advertisement, the newspaper-fed man who believes in progress, possibly even the rational dress of the future.[1]

Fig. 9.1. Tenniel. Alice in the railway carriage. From *Through the Looking-Glass.*

Empson apparently was looking at the picture here, not the text; for the text does not specify newspapers, but Tenniel's passenger does hold a newspaper—whatever he may be wearing.

On the next page, Empson hazarded that Disraeli "turns up again as the unicorn when the Lion and the Unicorn are fighting for the Crown." Probably this too refers to an illustration (fig. 1.50; which shows the combatants more clearly than the illustration of them actually at fisticuffs, a few pages before); in any case both of Empson's suggestions have been applied to the Tenniel illustrations.

Even Frances Sarzano, who was skeptical about other supposed "models" for various figures in *Alice*, was not prepared "to deny that the paper-clad passenger in the railway compartment is Benjamin Disraeli." As Martin Gardner put it in *The Annotated Alice*, "A comparison of the illustration of the man in white paper with Tenniel's political cartoons in *Punch* leaves little doubt that the face under the folded paper hat is Benjamin Disraeli's." Gardner went on to suggest that "Tenniel and/or Carroll may have had in mind the 'white paper' (official documents) with which such statesmen are surrounded." Donald J. Gray observed that "there is nothing in the text to make it appropriate that in Tenniel's drawing the man dressed in paper unmistakably resembles Benjamin Disraeli, unless it is his advice to take a return ticket every time the train stops"—construed to refer to Disraeli's hopes to regain the position of prime minister, which he lost to Gladstone in 1868.[2]

As regards the later illustration (fig. 1.50), if the Unicorn was Disraeli then the Lion might as well be Gladstone; and in 1945 Florence Becker Lennon suggested that he was, citing as evidence Tenniel's "cartoons of the two alternating Prime Ministers in *Punch*." Later Martin Gardner said that "it was widely believed in England" (when?) that this picture caricatured the two prime ministers, adding that although "there is no proof of this . . . they do resemble Tenniel's *Punch* car-

Fig. 9.2. Tenniel. Disraeli and Gladstone (cartoon detail). From *Punch*, 20 May 1871.

toons of the two political figures who often sparred with each other."[3]

Two related suggestions have not met with such wide acceptance. Roger Lancelyn Green has compared the Mad Hatter of *Alice's Adventures* (fig. 5.1) to Tenniel's Gladstone; and Alison Lurie has seen the contrast between the dapper Walrus and the proletarian Carpenter (fig. 1.25) to be a contrast betwen Disraeli and Gladstone.[4]

Most of these claims invite the reader to compare the *Alice* illustrations to typical Tenniel caricatures of the two prime ministers. So I have selected some representative cartoons from 1871 (the year that Tenniel finished drawing the *Looking-Glass* illustrations) as a basis for comparison. Figures 9.2, 9.3, 9.4, and 9.5 are details from contemporary cartoons that show the faces of both Disraeli (with the goatee) and Gladstone.[5] Disraeli's profile in these cartoons does roughly match the profile of the man in the paper hat; but in all of Tenniel's political cartoons there is a definite chin under the goatee, which itself is fairly well developed, whereas in the railway-car illustration the man in the paper hat has a receding chin and the merest wisp of a goatee. If Tenniel had wanted the engravers (the Dalziel brothers) to produce a likeness consistent with his *Punch* caricatures of Disraeli, he could easily have controlled these details. An early drawing of this scene shows the man in white paper both chinless and beardless (fig. 9.6).[6] It is unlikely that he is a deliberate caricature of Disraeli.

Fig. 9.3. Tenniel. Disraeli and Gladstone (cartoon detail). From *Punch*, 27 May 1871.

Fig. 9.4. Tenniel. Disraeli and Gladstone (cartoon detail). From *Punch*, 1 July 1871.

Fig. 9.6. Tenniel. Early sketch of Alice in the railway carriage. From Phillip James, *Children's Books of Yesterday* (1933).

Fig. 9.5. Tenniel. Disraeli and Gladstone (cartoon detail). From *Punch*, 5 August 1871.

Fig. 9.7. The royal arms. From Burke, *Peerage and Baronetage*, 31st ed. (1869).

Of course the Unicorn in figure 1.50 does have a conspicuous goatee; and I suspect that it was this detail that first prompted the identification with Disraeli. Certainly in no other respect does the Unicorn look much like Disraeli. But a goatee is part of the nature of the beast. According to tradition a unicorn is partly goatlike; and in British heraldry unicorns have goat beards, as in figure 9.7, a contemporary rendering of the royal arms.[7] So there is nothing peculiarly Disraeliesque about the Unicorn in figure 1.50.

The case for Gladstone is no better. The Lion in figure

1.50 is as dour as the Gladstone of figures 9.2, 9.3, and 9.4, but there is little else to compare. However, the Lion in figure 1.50 is indistinguishable from the adult lion in figure 9.8, also drawn by Tenniel in 1871, who represents not Gladstone but the ideal English paterfamilias.[8]

To allegorize the Lion and the Unicorn into Gladstone and Disraeli is a pleasant idea, but it was not Tenniel's or Carroll's.

A LESSON WORTH LEARNING.

"AND TEACH THE YOUNG IDEA HOW TO—SWIM!"

(*Hint to Sea-side Society.*)

Fig. 9.8 Tenniel. "A Lesson Worth Learning." From *Punch*, 7 October 1871.

The man in white paper, the goat, and the guard's use of binoculars are all bizarre details in figure 9.1; and yet Tenniel's drawing of the interior of the railway compartment presents, nonetheless, a more or less ordinary view. The lack of privacy to be had in even a first-class railway compartment was the basis for countless *Punch* cartoons during the fifties and sixties. For example, figure 9.9 (drawn by Gordon Thompson in 1861) shows a bohemian artist affronting a

ENTHUSIASTIC ARTIST. "*My dear Sir, keep that Expression for one moment! You've got such a splendid Head for my Picture of the 'Canting Hypocrite!'*"

Fig. 9.9. Gordon Thompson. "Enthusiastic Artist." From *Punch*, 15 June 1861.

straitlaced clergyman in a compartment much like Alice's. And figure 9.10 (unsigned, 1858) has a guard intrude on the privacy of the passengers almost as effectively as Tenniel's guard does in figure 9.1.[9] The indignities of railway travel are not much worse in the *Looking-Glass* illustration than they could be in fact.

And yet privacy was possible in such a setting, as can be seen in the handsome genre painting by Augustus Leopold Egg, *The Travelling Companions* (1862; fig. 9.11). The girl sleeping and the other girl reading are each in a private world, comfortably protected by yards of luxurious fabric, oblivious even to the picturesque foreign landscape passing outside their window. No guard menaces them, and no goat,

and no dubious man in white paper. But their compartment is virtually the same as Alice's, the posture of the girl on the right is the same, and even their little black hats are the same, each ornamented with a red feather, like Alice's white one.

As Raymond Lister suggests, Tenniel may have known this painting. A possible connection would be through John Leech or Mark Lemon of *Punch*, both mutual friends of Egg and Tenniel.[10] However, neither the mass-produced railway compartment nor the stylish porkpie hat were unusual sights in mid-Victorian times. Tenniel's title-page illustration for the first *Punch* volume of 1861 shows two such hats adorning young women several years older than Alice (fig. 9.12). Alice's hat—including a white feather—her barrel muff, her shoes, her skirt, and her general posture, all figure in J. E. Millais' sentimental and vastly popular genre painting *My*

A FACT.

Three Gentlemen Smoking in a Railway Carriage—Guard puts in his head, and loquitur: "*There are two things not allowed on this Line, Gentlemen; Smoking, and the Servants of the Company receiving Money.*" The result, a metallic pass from Gentlemen to Guard.

Fig. 9.10. "A Fact. Three Gentlemen Smoking in a Railway Carriage. . . ." From *Punch*, 23 October 1858.

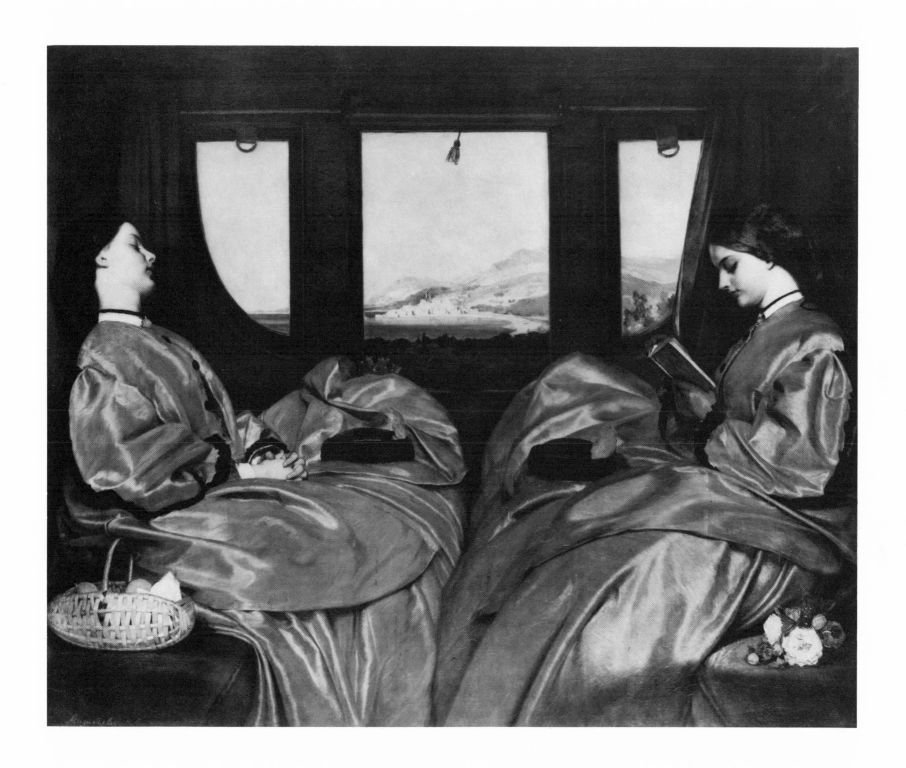

Fig. 9.11. Augustus Leopold Egg. *The Travelling Companions*. Painting.
Published by permission of the Birmingham Museum and Art Gallery.

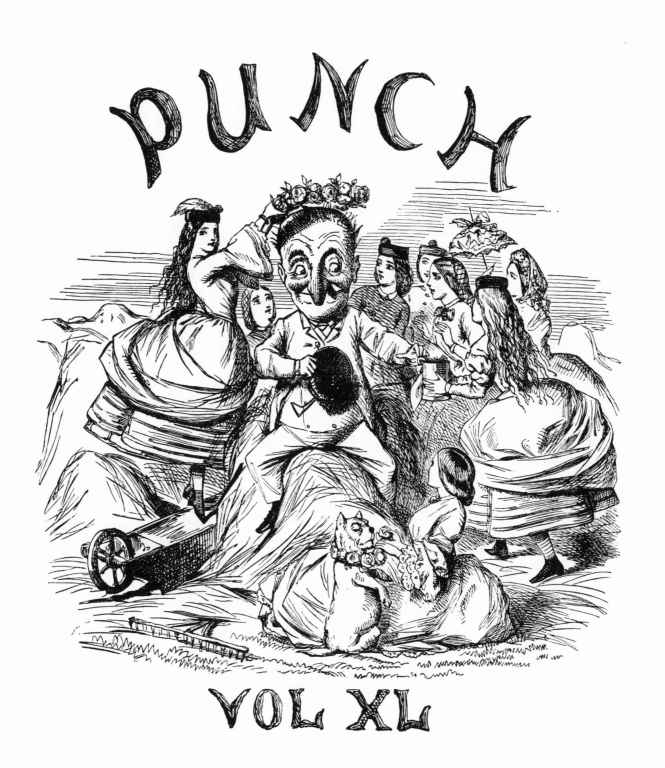

Fig. 9.12. Tenniel. Fashionable young women with Mr. Punch.
From *Punch*, January–June 1861.

Fig. 9.13. T. O. Barlow, after J. E. Millais. *My First Sermon*. Mixed mezzotint engraving. Crown Copyright Victoria and Albert Museum.

First Sermon, which was exhibited at the Royal Academy in 1863 and published as an engraving (fig. 9.13) in 1865.[11] In 1868 Tenniel put a similar hat on a girl he drew for *Punch* who could pass for Alice (fig. 9.14; she is shown on the edge of a crowd at the Zoological Gardens). This girl already has the striped stockings that Alice will wear in *Through the*

Fig. 9.14. Tenniel. Girl in striped stockings (cartoon detail). From *Punch's Almanack for 1868*.

Looking-Glass, a change from the plain ones of *Alice's Adventures*; and, like the Alice of figure 9.1, she still has the porkpie hat that had passed from adult fashion some years before. It is hard to say when this style ceased to be fashionable for little girls. A photograph of three young aristocratic sisters taken in 1871 (fig. 9.15) shows larger hats with bigger feathers; but otherwise Alice's traveling outfit was very much up to date when Tenniel drew it, despite his old-fashioned habits. The girl on the left could be Alice herself.[12]

Two illustrations in the same chapter of *Through the Looking-Glass* draw attention to an old-fashioned decorative motif that may seem mysterious if noticed out of historical context. Tenniel shows two of Carroll's "looking-glass insects" against a background of relatively large ivy leaves (fig. 8.15, 9.16). This compositional device draws attention to the ivy that flourishes elsewhere in this book: there is ivy on the oak tree in the frontispiece, ivy on the tree behind Tweedledum and Tweedledee, and a spray of ivy on Humpty Dumpty's wall. Ivy being an ancient symbol—variously of love, wine, victory, or mourning—one might wonder whether Tenniel was using ivy symbolically in *Through the Looking-Glass*, and, if so, how.

In fact the abundant ivy in *Through the Looking-Glass* is only decorative and not symbolic, a vestige of Tenniel's early graphic repertoire. Figures 9.17 and 9.18, early ornamental initials for *Punch*, integrate ivy and calligraphy in a way that recalls the little vines or "vinets" (vignettes) that decorate the borders and illustrated capitals of illuminated medieval manuscripts. Tenniel, having studied in Munich, was as susceptible as any Victorian artist to the vogue for German design, which in the second quarter of the nineteenth century revived elements of archaic page layout, including borders made up of ivy and other vines. (The various L-shaped illustrations in the *Alice* books, which integrate closely with the text alongside, are a product of the same design tradition.)[13] The German influence was widespread; figure 9.19 shows a representative engraved title page from the early fifties, framed with posts that are entwined with ivy. Tenniel used a similar framing device in illustrations for *Aesop's Fables* (1848; fig. 9.20) and Martin Tupper's *Proverbial Philosophy* (1854; fig. 9.21). This illustration, to Tupper's poem "Of Education," borrows more than the grape-arbor motif from D. G. Rossetti's famous first Pre-Raphaelite painting, *The Girlhood of Mary Virgin* (exhibited 1849; fig. 9.22).[14]

By the time, some two decades later, that Tenniel came to draw the illustrations to *Through the Looking-Glass*, the supporting posts were gone, and the ivy had become a more natural part of the landscape; but it remained a vestige of an essentially ornamental tradition.

Figure 9.19, the title page drawn by Henry Anelay and engraved by J. Johnston for *Aunt Jane's Verses for Children* by Mrs. T. D. Crewdson (1851; also 1855, 1871), relates to "Looking-Glass Insects" by virtue not only of its ornamental frame but also of its central subject. In the climactic scene of that chapter, after Alice has lost herself in a shadowy wood and forgotten the names of things, she comes upon an equally innocent fawn. For a moment the two share a rare idyll, which Tenniel illustrates in figure 9.23; it ends abruptly when the fawn discovers its natural identity:

So they walked on together through the wood, Alice with her arms clasped lovingly round the soft neck of the Fawn, till they came out into another open field, and here the Fawn gave a sudden bound into the air, and shook itself free from Alice's arms. "I'm a Fawn!" it cried out in a voice of delight, "and, dear me! you're a human child!" A sudden look of alarm came into its beautiful brown eyes, and in another moment it had darted away at full speed.

Fig. 9.15. Photograph of daughters of the fourth marquess of Bath. Reproduced by courtesy of the Marquess of Bath, Longleat House, Warminster, Wiltshire, England.

Fig. 9.16. Tenniel. Snap-dragon-fly. From *Through the Looking-Glass*.

Fig. 9.17. Tenniel. Ornamental initial. From *Punch*, January–June 1851.

Fig. 9.18. Tenniel. Ornamental initial. From *Punch*, January–June 1851.

Fig. 9.19. Henry Anelay. Illustrated title page. From Mrs. T. D. Crewdon, *Aunt Jane's Verses for Children* (1851).

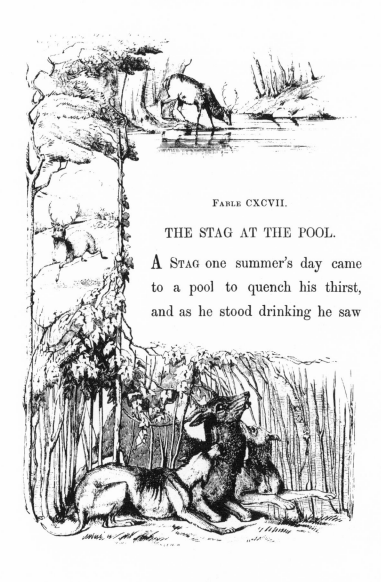

Fable CXCVII.

THE STAG AT THE POOL.

A Stag one summer's day came
to a pool to quench his thirst,
and as he stood drinking he saw

Fig. 9.20. Tenniel. "The Stag at the Pool." From *Aesop's Fables* (1848).

Fig. 9.21. Tenniel. "Of Education." From Martin Tupper, *Proverbial Philosophy* (1854; rpt. n.d.).

Fig. 9.22. Dante Gabriel Rossetti. *The Girlhood of Mary Virgin*. Painting. The Tate Gallery, London.

Fig. 9.23. Tenniel. Alice and the Fawn. From *Through the Looking-Glass*.

Thus Alice is bereft of one of the only two companions she will have on the other side of the looking-glass. (The other, the White Knight, shares a similar moment of sentiment with her in the dark of the forest; but he is too much like C. L. Dodgson to be as congenial a companion.) In exchange for this loss, Alice finds the recompense of language regained: "Alice stood looking after it, almost ready to cry with vexation at having lost her dear little fellow-traveller so suddenly. 'However, I know my name now,' she said, 'that's *some* comfort. Alice—Alice—I won't forget it again.' "

Alice's passing encounter with the world of natural innocence has a high romantic mood about it, the grand nostalgia of "Tintern Abbey," if transposed to a simpler key. The mood could easily have been one of low Victorian sentiment. The poem by Mrs. Crewdson that figure 9.19 illustrates, "The Fawn," describes a roughly similar encounter between some children and a fawn:

> He stood beside us, and his eyes,
>   So large, and black, and bright,
> Did seem to speak of kind surprise,
>   And fondness and delight.
>
> . . . .
>
> He rubb'd his little silky nose
>   Against my cheek and hand,
> And look'd as if he'd like to *coze*,
>   So kind he seem'd, and bland!

Unlike Carroll's fawn this one does *not* actually "coze" (converse in a friendly or familiar way); also, the children disappoint it by carrying only wild flowers, nothing worth eating. In the end, like Carroll's fawn, the animal remembers its true nature—unfortunately sentimentalized by Mrs. Crewdson into an image of motherhood:

> Oh spotted fawn! Oh speckled fawn!
>   He sees a soft eye glisten,
> And there, across the grassy lawn,
>   An ear is pricked to listen.
>
> He sees that ear, he knows that eye,
>   (There dare approach no other)
> Away his glinting footsteps fly,
>   *It is the doe,—his mother!*

In this poem neither the fawn nor the children are ever alone. Their encounter might almost as well take place in a children's zoo as in the wild. The easy vulgarity of both this poem and Anelay's illustration emphasize by contrast the sober dignity of both Carroll's scene and Tenniel's drawing.

CHAPTER TEN

Carroll and Tenniel in Collaboration

How much control did Carroll exercise over Tenniel's illustrations for the *Alice* books? What elements of the pictures did Tenniel determine himself? The historical record is relatively thin; furthermore, parts of it are ambiguous, and others are apocryphal. I will review it in this chapter; and in the next will consider some practical and theoretical aspects of Victorian book illustration, before assessing there the implications of the previous chapters.

Most of the little that is certain about Tenniel's work on the first book, *Alice's Adventures*, is recorded in Carroll's diaries. Chapter 2 has already drawn upon some of this material, but other details are worth noticing. For one thing it appears to have been Carroll's practice to forward to Tenniel galley proofs of the text to be illustrated as soon as they became available from the printers.[1] It is therefore likely that Tenniel from the start drew his illustrations with reference to the enlarged text of *Alice's Adventures in Wonderland*, rather than the original, shorter text of *Alice's Adventures under Ground*, even though it is evident that he also had access at some time to Carroll's illustrations to the original version.

Another detail, itself minor, takes on interest in the light of later events. On 21 June 1864, Carroll visited his publisher, Macmillan, "who strongly advised my altering the size of the page of my book, and adopting that of *The Water Babies*," by Charles Kingsley—published by Macmillan the previous year. That same day Carroll "called on Tenniel, who agreed to the change of page." Evidently Carroll was willing to be advised by Tenniel about details of book design even at this early stage of their collaboration (Tenniel had not yet started work on the pictures). Carroll's deference foreshadowed one of the most famous incidents in the history of book publishing.

The story has often been told how Carroll suppressed the first printing of *Alice's Adventures* because (as Carroll put it) Tenniel was "entirely dissatisfied with the printing of the pictures" (*Diaries*, 1: 234). In a careful analysis of the in-

cident, W. H. Bond has concluded that the defects of the first printing were subtle but real. They were of several kinds; but the most significant from Tenniel's point of view would have been the careless press work that diminished the contrast between the light and dark areas of a picture. (Bond cites Tenniel's instructions in a contemporary letter to George Dalziel about an unrelated engraving, in which he calls for a full range of tones.) Tenniel was not being captious in objecting to the printing, and Carroll was not being over-finicky in commissioning (at his own expense) a wholly new printing of the book. However, the defects of the first printing were subtle enough that Carroll, inexperienced in such matters, would not have objected if it weren't for Tenniel's objections. In the letter to Dalziel already mentioned, Tenniel recalled: "I protested so strongly against the disgraceful printing, that he *cancelled the edition*."[2]

In the end almost all the copies from the defective printing were outfitted with new title pages and unloaded on the American market—after Carroll dutifully asked for and got Tenniel's permission. This arrangement helped make up for the cost of the new printing. But the new printing cost Carroll time as well as money, and there is a touch of exasperation in his first diary entry on the subject: "I suppose we shall have to do it all again."[3] The delay for reprinting amounted to five months.

This major delay was not the first that Tenniel caused. Although Carroll originally wanted to publish the book in time for Christmas 1864, Tenniel was slow to begin work. On 20 June, over two and a half months after Tenniel had accepted the commission, Carroll found that he had "not begun the pictures yet." On 20 November Carroll wrote to Macmillan: "I fear my little book *Alice's Adventures in Wonderland* cannot appear this year. Mr. Tenniel writes that he is hopeless of completing the pictures by Xmas. The cause I do not know, but he writes in great trouble, having just lost his mother, and I have begged him to put the thing aside for the present."[4] Apparently Carroll thought Tenniel had been delaying even before the current crisis. The rest of the letter to Macmillan indicates that he now hoped for publication in time for Easter, if not sooner.

Within a month Tenniel did send Carroll the first twelve proofs from the engraved blocks, but the last ones did not arrive until 18 June. By 15 July there were "twenty or more" copies of the completed book available to Carroll at Macmillan's, which he inscribed to friends with a feeling of satisfaction that can be guessed at. Four days later Carroll heard from Tenniel that the printing was unacceptable.[5]

Two important facts about Tenniel and *Alice's Adventures* are implied by this series of events. One is that Tenniel conceived his *Alice* illustrations in terms of a full chiaroscuro, placing considerable demands upon his printer. (If Tenniel was disturbed by the way the first printing muffled the contrast of his pictures, he would be appalled by the way that they appear in many modern mass-paperback editions). The other implication is that Tenniel was not a mere servant or tool commissioned to carry out Carroll's pictorial intentions: from the start he commanded authority in the collaborative relationship, and he did not hesitate to exercise it.

Three other stories more directly involve the imagery of Tenniel's drawings for *Alice's Adventures*, but they require close scrutiny.

Fifty years ago H. W. Greene wrote a letter to the *Times* asserting that Carroll had Tenniel model his drawing of the Mad Hatter on one Theophilus Carter, an Oxford cabinetmaker and furniture dealer, who was remembered as the inventor of a "clockwork bed" displayed at the Exhibition of 1851. This bed, an invention worthy of the White Knight himself, "tipped up and threw the occupant out at the appointed hour." According to Greene, Carter "was the doubtless unconscious model for the Mad Hatter in 'Through the Looking-Glass' [sic] as depicted by Tenniel, who was brought down to Oxford by the author, as I have heard, on purpose to see him. The likeness was unmistakable."

A few days later, the Reverend W. Gordon Baillie disputed the notion that Carter did not know he had been the model for the Mad Hatter. His letter is a genial mix of hearsay, surmise, fair play, and condescension:

> Your correspondent, Mr. H.W. Greene, thinks that Theophilus Carter was unaware that he figured in "Through the Looking Glass" [sic].

But all Oxford called him "The Mad Hatter," and surely his friends, or enemies, must have chaffed him about it. He would stand at the door of his furniture shop in the High, sometimes in an apron, always with a top-hat at the back of his head, which, with a well-developed nose and a somewhat receding chin, made him an easy target for the caricaturist. The story went that Mr. Dodgson ("Lewis Carroll"), thinking T. C. had imposed upon him, took this revenge. In justice to the man's memory, I may say that I possess a carved oak armchair which I bought from him, second-hand, 50 years ago. It is as good as ever, and the price was very moderate.

As a cap to this correspondence, W. J. Ryland, who had originally mentioned Carter in connection with the clockwork bed, testified that he had not known "that Carter was the original of the 'Mad Hatter,' but on looking again at the Tenniel drawing I see it is he to the life. To me," he went on, introducing a red herring, "he was the living image of the late W. E. Gladstone, and, being well aware of the fact, was always careful to wear the high collar and black stock so often depicted in *Punch* in cartoons of the 'Grand Old Man.' "[6]

All three witnesses agreed that Carter looked like Tenniel's Mad Hatter, and according to Baillie the resemblance was widely noticed. But the explanation of this resemblance is obviously hearsay ("as I have heard"; "the story went"). In the last fifty years, the Carter legend has often been retold, but no evidence has come to light, in Carroll's diaries, letters, or elsewhere, that Carroll ever brought Tenniel to Oxford for any purpose. Until some such evidence does turn up, the legend should be rejected.[7]

Also fifty years ago, shortly after Greene publicized the Theophilus Carter story, Falconer Madan publicized the more interesting and even more influential claim that Tenniel modeled his drawings of Alice on a young girl named Mary Hilton Badcock. Carroll, supposedly taken with a photograph of Miss Badcock (fig. 10.1), was thought to have purchased a copy in January 1865, which he "recommended" to Tenniel. (We now know what Madan may not have known: that Tenniel and Dalziel had by this time already completed a dozen engravings; see note 5 above.) According to Madan, Tenniel "subsequently paid visits" to the girl's home at Ripon "and adopted the suggestion." For this information as well as for a copy of the photograph, Madan was indebted to the adult Mary Badcock (now Mrs. W. G. C. Probert) and to her husband. "The resemblance," Madan wrote with circumspect indefiniteness, "is stated to be even closer in the *Looking-Glass* than in the earlier volume."[8]

This story has had a mixed reception. Roger Lancelyn

Fig. 10.1. Photograph of Mary Hilton Badcock. From S. H. Williams and F. Madan, *A Handbook of the Literature of the Rev. C. L. Dodgson (Lewis Carroll)* (1931).

Green and Denis Crutch silently dropped it—photograph and all—from their later editions of Madan's *Handbook*. Carroll's recent biographers have taken it up with more or less caution. Florence Becker Lennon, John Pudney, Derek Hudson, and Anne Clark all say or imply that Carroll did send Tenniel this photograph, which all publish as an illustration (Clark, in her biography of Alice Liddell). Hudson, partly because of the chronological problem, doubts that Tenniel paid the photograph any attention. Clark sees little resemblance "except for the long blonde hair," though in the Liddell biography she implies that Tenniel did make Alice a blonde because of the photograph.

In the first edition of *The Illustrators of Alice*, Graham Ovenden printed the photograph too, with the caption, "Mary Hilton Badcock, the model for Tenniel's Alice." Florence Becker Lennon not only saw a resemblance between the photograph and the picture but repeated the story of Tenniel making "several trips to Ripon to sketch" the girl. And yet, later in her book Lennon quotes from a partly unpublished letter of Carroll's, written to Gertrude Thomson, an artist and illustrator with whom he began to correspond in 1878:

> Mr. Tenniel is the only artist, who has drawn for me, who has resolutely refused to use a model, and declared he no more needed one than I should need a multiplication table to work a mathematical problem! I venture to think that he was mistaken, & that for want of a model, he drew several pictures of "Alice" entirely out of proportion—head decidedly too large and feet decidedly too small.[9]

So Tenniel didn't travel to Ripon to sketch any model. I think that Green and Crutch were right to drop the whole Badcock story from their *Handbook*. There is no disinterested authority for it, and the photograph does not look any more like Alice than do Tenniel's other renderings of young English girls (see figs. 1.44, 9.12, 9.14).

Without any photograph it is hard to judge directly the competing claim that has been made by the granddaughter of Mark Lemon, the first editor of *Punch*. She believed that Tenniel used her mother, Kate Lemon, as a model for Alice. Kate was eight years old in 1864, when Tenniel is supposed to have chosen her as a model. According to Arthur Adrian, it was a family tradition that "posing for her pictures was not an altogether happy experience, for she hated the striped stockings which Tenniel made her wear. Once the sittings were finished, they disappeared mysteriously through a crack in the staircase." But Alice doesn't wear striped stockings in *Alice's Adventures*: only in *Looking-Glass*. In 1871, when Tenniel illustrated the later book, Kate Lemon was fifteen years old—twice the age of the fictional *Alice*. This tradition seems no more reliable than the Badcock tradition.[10]

If Tenniel's Alice had any prototype, aside from Tenniel's customary representations of middle-class girls, it was Carroll's Alice: not the historical Alice Liddell, of course, who was dark-haired and wore bangs (fig. 10.2), but the Alice that

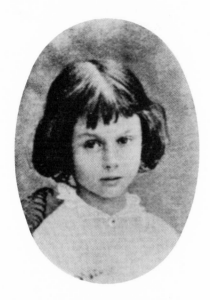

Fig. 10.2. Carroll. Photograph of Alice Liddell. By permission of the British Library.

Carroll drew himself in the gift manuscript. Jeffrey Stern has shown that the Alice of Carroll's drawings embodies Pre-Raphaelite notions of feminine beauty, especially as expressed by the painters Arthur Hughes and Dante Gabriel Rossetti.[11] Some of this influence carries over to Tenniel's conception, though he moderates it considerably. Tenniel combs Alice's abundant hair back, instead of parting it, and he minimizes the Pre-Raphaelite wave. (In *Looking-Glass* he adds a hairband—which, thanks to him, became known as an "Alice band.") Aside from the long hair, the most important trait that Tenniel takes from Carroll's drawings of Alice is the impassive, almost pouty expression. Another mark of Pre-Raphaelite style, it suits the sober child described in the text.

Within a year of the publication of *Alice's Adventures*, Carroll confided to Macmillan that he had "a floating idea of writing a sort of sequel to *Alice*."[12] His first task was to commission an illustrator. Presumably he approached Tenniel first—most likely in the fall or winter of 1866. As late as April 1868, Tenniel was still resisting the idea, pleading lack of time (*Diaries*, 2: 267).

Early in 1867 Carroll turned to Richard Doyle, a popular illustrator, whom Tenniel had long since replaced on the staff of *Punch*. Falconer Madan says that Carroll wrote to Doyle on 22 January 1867, "by Tenniel's advice."[13] Two days later Carroll visited Doyle, who was interested in the project but uncertain that he could do it in time. "We left the matter unsettled for the present," Carroll recorded (*Diaries*, 1: 249). A year later he was writing to Mrs. George MacDonald, "Doyle isn't good enough (look at any of his later pictures)."[14] By then he was in real difficulty, having just been turned down by Sir Joseph Noël Paton, the illustrator of Kingsley's *Water Babies* (Macmillan & Co., 1863), and a well-known painter of fairy and allegorical subjects. Paton, who seems to have been another nominee of Tenniel's (*Diaries*, 2:267), pleaded ill health, and insisted in any case that Tenniel was the man for the job. Carroll wrote to Tenniel once more, making the remarkable offer to "pay his publishers for his time for the next five months. Unless he will undertake it, I am quite at a loss" (*Diaries*, 2:269). A month later, in June 1868, Tenniel agreed to do the illustrations to the new book, but only "at such spare times as he can find" (*Diaries*, 2:270).

Some months later Carroll noted that Tenniel "reluctantly consented, as his hands are full: I have tried Noel Paton and Proctor in vain" (*Diaries*, 2:275). "Proctor" must be John Proctor, an artist now almost entirely forgotten, who from September 1867 until December 1868 was the chief cartoonist for *Judy, or the London Serio-Comic Journal*.[15] This new weekly magazine, which very closely mimicked the format of *Punch*, featured a large political cartoon drawn by Proctor in Tenniel's heroic-allegorical style. Carroll must have hoped that Proctor's knack for imitating Tenniel could be applied to the second *Alice* book. But Proctor turned down this chance to enter literary history, and in the end the real Tenniel agreed to do the job.[16]

As Tenniel had warned, progress was slow. Although Carroll had sent the first chapter of *Looking-Glass* to the printer in January 1869, Tenniel had not started on the drawings by early April. "Rough sketches of about ten of the pictures" were available for inspection in January of the following year, and printed proofs of seven by late June. On 15 January 1871, Carroll sent the last proofs of *Looking-Glass* to Tenniel, noting that "it all now depends upon him, whether we get the book out by Easter or not." After more delays on Tenniel's part forced Carroll to defer his hopes from Easter to midsummer, and then to Michaelmas, he finally reconciled himself to Christmas, when the book did appear.

The information on record about Carroll's and Tenniel's negotiations over the second book is more specific than that for the first. Collingwood preserved two details as examples of how closely Carroll controlled—or tried to control—Tenniel's work: "Mr. Dodgson was no easy man to work with; no detail was too small for his exact criticism. 'Don't give Alice so much crinoline,' he would write, or 'The White Knight must not have whiskers; he must not be made to look old'—such were the directions he was constantly giving."[17] Assuming that this generalization applies to *Alice's Adventures* as well as to *Looking-Glass*, it helps account for Tenniel's reluctance to take on the second book, despite the popular success of the first.

Carroll's remark about excessive crinoline probably refers to the crinoline-supported chessmanlike skirt of the dress that Tenniel originally gave Alice on her becoming Queen; it has the general shape of the carved skirts worn by the Red Queen and the White Queen, though it is more obviously made of soft fabric, real clothing for a real person. Proofs survive of all five *Looking-Glass* engravings that show Queen Alice, in both the uncorrected and the corrected states of the woodblocks. Figures 10.3 and 10.4 typify what Carroll was objecting to, and figures 1.43 and 1.17 what Tenniel supplied instead. The replacement is a more conventional formal dress for a young girl of the period (compare figure 9.15), and not so full as the chessman outfit.[18]

Tenniel ignored the other instruction that Collingwood cites, however. Despite Carroll's objections, Tenniel's White Knight kept his long whiskers and looks quite old—not a flattering self-image for Carroll, who modeled much of the Knight's character on himself. In the end, according to the evidence of chapter 6, Tenniel's White Knight wound up looking just like Ponny Mayhew.

But Collingwood's general point, that Carroll strictly supervised Tenniel's work, finds support elsewhere, in the recollections of Harry Furniss. Furniss, a younger *Punch* col-

Fig. 10.3. Tenniel. Rejected version (in proof) of figure 1.43. By permission of the British Museum.

Fig. 10.4. Tenniel. Rejected version (in proof) of figure 1.17. By permission of the British Museum.

league of Tenniel's, illustrated Carroll's two *Sylvie and Bruno* books (1889, 1893). He found Carroll to be "a captious critic."

> He subjected every illustration, when finished, to a minute examination under a magnifying glass. He would take a square inch of the drawing, count the lines I had made in that space, and compare their number with those on a square inch of illustration made for "Alice" by Tenniel! And in due course I would receive a long essay on the subject from Dodgson the mathematician.

One such dispute led Carroll to tell Furniss that he intended to write an article or pamphlet called "Authors' Difficulties with Illustrators." This pamphlet was never written, but no doubt Tenniel was partly responsible for the idea. It corresponds to an angry squib called "Authors and Booksellers" or "The Profits of Authorship" that Carroll planned but seems never to have published. The similarity of these vengeful projects suggests that Carroll was as much of a trial to his illustrators as he notoriously was to his publishers.[19]

According to Furniss, Tenniel lost all patience with Carroll's niggling interference, and afterwards dismissed him as "that conceited old Don." "When I told Tenniel that I had been approached by Dodgson to illustrate his books, he said, 'I'll give you a week, old chap; *you* will never put up with that fellow a day longer. . . . Lewis Carroll is impossible.' "[20] Furniss's memoir has the air of casual exaggeration; but even allowing for exaggeration it is clear that Carroll was a difficult author for an illustrator to work with.

And yet Carroll was willing to make major and minor changes in *Looking-Glass* to satisfy Tenniel. He told Furniss himself about one instance. When Tenniel unaccountably "remonstrated against the walrus and the carpenter as a hopeless combination, and begged to have the 'Carpenter' abolished—I remember offering 'baronet' and 'butterfly' . . . but he finally chose 'Carpenter'."[21] Tenniel had a more decisive effect on the lines, "The Walrus and the Carpenter / Were walking close at hand," which Carroll revised, "to suit the artist," from the original reading: "Were walking hand-in-hand" (*Letters*, 1:222). Carroll doesn't mention Tenniel's reason for objecting; but the Walrus, as Tenniel drew him, has flippers that look like flippers—not hands.

Collingwood records two letters in which Tenniel suggested other changes that Carroll adopted. The more impor-

tant of these concerned an extended passage in *Looking-Glass*, one that both Tenniel and Collingwood called a "chapter," perhaps mistakenly. It featured a wasp in a wig. At some point Tenniel objected that "a *wasp* in a *wig* is altogether beyond the appliances of art." And toward the end of a letter dated 1 June 1870, which Collingwood reproduced in facsimile (fig. 10.5), Tenniel expanded on his feelings: "Don't think me brutal, but I am bound to say that the '*wasp*' chapter doesn't interest me in the least, & I can't see my way to a picture. If you want to shorten the book, I can't help thinking—with all submission—that *there* is your opportunity." Whether Carroll thought Tenniel brutal or not, he took his advice, and there is no wasp in any wig in *Through the Looking-Glass*. However, Carroll's own marked-up galleys of the episode have recently been discovered and published, and the slackness of the entire episode justifies Tenniel's critical judgment, and Carroll's willingness to go along with it.[22]

At the start of the same letter, Tenniel provided Carroll with a rough sketch of the railway-carriage illustration, and suggested that when the carriage suddenly leaps into the air Alice should grab hold of the goat's beard, "instead of the old lady's hair." Tenniel left the old lady out of his sketch, and Carroll obligingly dropped her from the chapter.

Taken together, all the evidence suggests that the Carroll-Tenniel collaboration was by no means one-sided. Both men could be demanding, and both sensibly found ways to accomodate the other's demands.

The effort exhausted both of them. Each remained active and continued to do successful work: Tenniel, his *Punch* cartoons; Carroll, *The Hunting of the Snark* (1876). But after collaborating with Tenniel, Carroll's gift for story-telling flagged—despite the great length of *Sylvie and Bruno* and its sequel. And Tenniel, who before working for Carroll had contributed illustrations to dozens of books—five of them illustrated entirely by him—did virtually no such work after 1872. When Carroll approached him to illustrate some new book of his (not since identified), Tenniel responded with honest detachment: "It is a curious fact that with 'Through the Looking-Glass' the faculty of making drawings for book illustration departed from me, and, notwithstanding all sorts of tempting inducements, I have done nothing in that direction since."[23]

Interior of Railway carriage.
(1st Class). Alice on seat
by herself. Man in white
paper, reading, & Goat.
very shadowy & indistinct
sitting opposite. (with opera-glass,)
looking in at windows.

My dear Dodgson.

I think that where
the jump occurs in the
Railway Scene you might
very well make Alice lay
hold of the Goat's beard
as being the object nearest
to her hand — instead of
the old lady's hair. The

jerk would naturally
throw them together.
Don't think me brutal, but
I am bound to say that
the 'wasp' chapter doesn't
interest me in the least; &
that I can't see my way
to a picture. If you
want to shorten the book,
I can't help thinking —
with all submission —
that there is your oppor-
tunity.
In an agony of haste
Yours sincerely
J Tenniel.

Portsdown Road.
June 1. 1870

Fig. 10.5. Letter from Tenniel to Carroll. From S. D. Collingwood, *The Life and Letters of Lewis Carroll (Rev. C. L. Dodgson)* (1898; rpt. 1899).

CHAPTER ELEVEN

Illustration and Difference

Alice's Adventures and *Through the Looking-Glass* are the most popular illustrated books to come down to us from the nineteenth century. Indeed, they are probably the only such books to have kept a very wide audience. But in their day they were not so remarkable. The publishing era called "the sixties," which actually spanned two decades, from 1855 to about 1875, was the golden age of illustration in England for both books and magazines; and in such a context the publication of each *Alice* book was a relatively minor event.[1]

Most sixties illustrations were produced by a centuries-old process known as wood engraving; more precisely, by a modern version of that process that was geared to the production of printed facsimiles of ink or pencil drawings. There was usually a division of labor: the artist would prepare a drawing for the professional engraver to cut into the end grain of a hardwood block (usually boxwood). The cutting would be done so that the lines of the drawing would stand out on the block in relief against the cut-away background; after being inked these relief lines would print black on a white ground, reproducing the original drawing.

For reasons to be mentioned shortly, this procedure had real commercial advantages, making its use widespread. And it did contribute to some illustrated books of remarkable merit. But despite its commercial and aesthetic vogue, Ruskin harshly criticized the technique. For the apparently continuous, freehand lines in such engravings, including the many squiggles and crosshatchings that closely mimicked the shaded areas of drawings, were cruelly deceptive. They resulted not from continuous cuts by the engraver's chisel but rather, as a sort of residue, from scores of minute, cramped, repetitive gouges into the surface of the block. Examining a small patch of crosshatched shadow in a typical wood engraving of the period (it happened to be a *Punch* cartoon by Tenniel), Ruskin calculated more than a thousand interstices, each requiring ten or so individual cuts. With characteristic moral fervor, he decried the mechanical, alienated nature of such work, and compared its commercial exploitation to the slave trade. Ruskin raised this cry in 1872, the same year *Looking-Glass* was published. Certainly few readers of the *Alice* books, then or now, have supposed that each illustration cost a craftsman hours and hours of niggling and tedious hand labor.[2]

In facsimile engraving of this sort it was usual for the artist to draw the intended picture—reversed left to right—directly onto the woodblock. (To heighten contrast the surface of the block would have been painted with whitewash.) The engraver then cut away the unmarked areas of the wood. But Tenniel followed a different procedure: he first prepared a sketch on regular paper, and then transferred the outlines of that sketch (in reverse) onto the whitewashed block using tracing paper, before elaborating the drawing on the block with a hard lead pencil. Such, at least, was his usual practice in drawing for *Punch*.[3]

For the *Alice* illustrations, Tenniel also prepared finely detailed drawings on Bristol board; it may have been from these that he made the outline tracings that he transferred to the block.[4] However, it is not clear why Tenniel finished these drawings in such fine detail. Perhaps they were for Carroll to approve, before Tenniel undertook the more critical task of finishing the drawing on the block. Conceivably, Tenniel also sent them to Dalziel, to supplement—or possibly even to supply the lack of—finely detailed drawings on the wood.[5]

The resulting engraved block was so durable as to make possible mass reproduction of the image—an improvement on the engraved copper plates that were common in eighteenth-century printing, which quickly suffered wear. Furthermore, being a relief and not intaglio process, wood engraving did not need special treatment. A copper or steel engraving had to be printed separately, even if on a sheet of paper shared with the text, because the paper had to be dampened to take the ink from the engraved plate; but a relief wood engraving could be printed along with the composed type on unprepared paper, making it much easier for the printer to integrate the pictures into the text. It will be seen in the next chapter how the early editions of the *Alice* books took advantage of this flexibility.

The fact that the engraved image stood out in relief on the woodblock also made it possible to make electrotype replicas of the blocks. The electrotypes could then be used in the actual printing, instead of the original blocks; this was in fact done for both *Alice* books, so that the woodblocks survive without significant wear. They are still owned by Macmillan, Carroll's original publisher.

For publishers, much of the appeal of wood engraving was economic; but from the time of Thomas Bewick the artistic possibilities of the medium were also attractive. "Serious" artists were not above drawing for it, and many engravers raised the mechanical side of the business almost to a high art. The most distinguished firm of engravers was that commonly known as the Brothers Dalziel—George and Edward Dalziel, assisted by two other brothers, a sister, and other employees. The firm engraved pictures for scores of illustrated books during the second half of the nineteenth century, and often produced and printed illustrated books for others to publish.[6] It was the Dalziels who prepared Tenniel's blocks for the *Alice* books.

The most celebrated book of "the sixties" is the illustrated edition of Tennyson's *Poems*, a deluxe reprint of the text of 1842, which Edward Moxon published in 1857. The book was not a great financial success, and it was not a uniform artistic success either. Although one of the virtues of wood engraving was the contribution it could make to unified layout, it was too common to waste this opportunity by commissioning for the same book drawings by different artists, and to have them engraved by different engravers. Such was the case with the Moxon illustrated Tennyson, which included illustrations by established artists (Thomas Creswick, William Mulready, Daniel Maclise, Clarkson Stanfield), and also work by younger, more remarkable members of the Pre-Raphaelite Brotherhood: John Everett Millais, William Holman Hunt, and Dante Gabriel Rossetti. The fifty-four engravings were done by six firms, with fifteen being produced in the Dalziel workshop.[7]

According to tradition Tennyson recommended the three Pre-Raphaelite artists to Moxon, and Maclise also; but beyond that, unlike Lewis Carroll, he had little if anything to do with designing the illustrations. However, he did criticize some of them after the fact; and his criticisms express one contemporary standard by which sixties book illustrations were judged.

Tennyson's opinion has been recorded most fully as regards Wiliam Holman Hunt's illustration for "The Lady of Shalott," which was engraved by John Thompson (fig. 11.1).

Fig. 11.1. William Holman Hunt. "The Lady of Shalott." From Moxon's illustrated edition of Tennyson's *Poems* (1857; rpt. 1866, 1976).

It became the best known illustration in the book, and indeed is one of the most remarkable engravings of the century. Hunt shows the Lady at the climactic moment of Tennyson's poem, when she has just renounced her world of innocent, dreamy, and artistic shadows for an unmediated and fatal view of the real world, a world made attractive by the erotic figure of Sir Lancelot. At that moment the tapestry she has been weaving tears asunder, and the mirror, which until then has mediated all her worldly experience, is also broken:

> Out flew the web and floated wide;
> The mirror crack'd from side to side.

It happens that the Lady's crisis resembles three different crises in the *Alice* books: one at the end of *Alice's Adventures*, when the deck of cards flies apart and Alice wakes abruptly from her dream (fig. 11.2); another at the end of *Through the* *Looking-Glass*, when Alice tears the tablecloth off the table and the candelabra explode into Roman candles, ending another dream (fig. 1.30); and the preliminary crisis in *Alice's Adventures* when Alice upsets the jury box—the crisis which, as drawn by Tenniel (fig. 11.3), approaches most closely to the style and composition of Hunt's engraving.[8]

Fig. 11.3. Tenniel. Alice upsetting the jury box. From *Alice's Adventures in Wonderland*.

Fig. 11.2. Tenniel. Alice and deck of cards. From *Alice's Adventures in Wonderland*.

When Tennyson visited Hunt's studio some time after the book appeared, he objected to the way that Hunt had drawn the broken tapestry: "Why did you make the web wind round and round her like the threads of a cocoon?" Hunt quoted the couplet given above as a justification. Tennyson insisted: "But I did not say it floated round and round her." He was offended also by Hunt's treatment of the Lady's hair, "wildly tossed about as if by a tornado." Hunt argued that this effect communicated her experience of the event, so that "while she recognised that the moment of the catastrophe had come, the spectator might also understand it"—and also, presumably, understand that she understood it. But Tennyson was not to be persuaded: "I didn't say that her hair was blown about like that." He thought it a general rule that "the illustrator should always adhere to the words of the poet," and that he "ought never to add anything to what he finds in the text." It was no use for Hunt to plead that poetry and drawing operated under different constraints, and that an illustration could not express anything like the same content as a poetic text except by interpreting it freely. "May I not urge that I had only half a page on which to convey the impression of weird fate, whereas you use about fifteen pages to give expression to the complete idea?"[9]

Dante Gabriel Rossetti, who contributed five illustrations to the volume, including the other illustration to "The Lady of Shalott," differed from Tennyson even more sharply than Hunt as regards the proper relation of illustration to text. Before he had started work on any of the illustrations, he commented to a friend that he wanted to illustrate poems whose meaning was implicit rather than explicit, poems like Tennyson's "*Vision of Sin* and *Palace of Art*, etc.,—those where one can allegorize on one's own hook on the subject of the poem, without killing, for oneself and everyone, a distinct idea of the poet's."[10] The vaguer the poem, the better the potential for a picture.

John Ruskin, Rossetti's mentor and ally, expressed a similar but even bolder theory in a letter that he wrote to Tennyson after the book was published:

> Many of the plates are very noble things, though not, it seems to me, illustrations of your poems.
> I believe, in fact, that good pictures never can be; they are always another poem, subordinate but wholly different from the poet's conception, and serve chiefly to show the reader how variously the same verses may affect various minds.[11]

Although Ruskin has poetry specifically in mind here, his argument applies just as well to prose fiction.

If taken yet one more step, however, the case for interpretive freedom can turn, ironically, *against* the illustrator—who then appears not as an imaginative reader of the author's text but rather as a usurper of the actual reader's own imaginative claims. So Graham Greene has regretted the "disservice" done to Dickens by illustrators such as George Cruikshank: "For no character any more will walk for the first time into our memory as we ourselves imagine him, and *our* imagination after all has just as much claim to truth as Cruikshank's."[12] Such a complaint could be made against *any* illustrations of Tennyson's poetry, Rossetti's included. And

Tenniel's *Alice* illustrations: are they objectionable on these grounds? They do compel the reader's imagination; but probably illustrations for the *Alice* books will always be privileged, thanks to Alice's own instinctive demand that a worthwhile book must have "pictures."

In the end, true to his prediction, Rossetti did draw two illustrations for Tennyson's visionary "The Palace of Art." One of these greatly perplexed the poet. Figure 11.4 is his interpretation of a tapestry that hung in the palace:

Fig. 11.4. Dante Gabriel Rossetti. St. Cecilia. From Moxon's illustrated edition of Tennyson's *Poems* (1857; rpt. 1866, 1976).

in a clear-wall'd city on the sea,
Near gilded organ-pipes, her hair
Wound with white roses, slept St. Cecily;
An angel look'd at her.

Aside from Rossetti's invention of much detail that is not defined by the text, there is the obvious discrepancy between the angel described in the poem, who merely "looked at" St. Cecilia, and his counterpart in the engraving, who is vigorously kissing her forehead. Rossetti's brother and biographer, William Michael Rossetti, years later conceded that in preparing the Moxon illustrations Rossetti "himself only, and not Tennyson, was his guide. . . . The illustration of *St. Cecilia* puzzled [Tennyson] not a little, and he had to give up the problem of what it had to do with his verses."[13]

Besides the topical discrepancy between the text and the engraving, there was another kind of discrepancy, between what Rossetti actually drew on the block and what Dalziel engraved there. By coincidence Lewis Carroll was an early critic of the difference between Rossetti's drawing and the Dalziel engraving. In 1859, before he met Rossetti, Carroll visited the artist's studio, and he reported his visit in a letter to Tennyson's wife, whom he had met a few years before. He there "saw photographs from the original drawings of *St. Cecily* and *The Lady of Shalott*. The difference between them and the woodcuts is certainly very striking."[14]

On the other hand, Tenniel's own finished drawings for *Alice* show that the Dalziel Brothers were capable of almost exact facsimile engraving—if it is right, that is, to assume that the Dalziels worked from these drawings, and that they were not meant for some other purpose (see above). The drawing and the engraving of Alice upsetting the jury box provide, in that case, a good example of how faithful a Dalziel engraving could be (see figs. 11.5 and 11.3, respectively).[15] In their memoir the Dalziels themselves acknowledged that when the *Alice* books were being prepared Carroll would find fault with both the drawings and the engravings; but they also implied that there was no lasting dissatisfaction on his part. When Carroll sent the Dalziels payment for their work on *Looking-Glass*, he did compliment them in terms that seem to be more than *pro forma*, despite being cast in the formal third-person idiom of business correspondence: "Mr. Dodgson encloses to Messrs. Dalziel a cheque for £203 16*s.*, in payment of their account, and takes the opportunity of thanking them for the great pains which have evidently been bestowed on the pictures. He thinks them quite admirable

Fig. 11.5. Tenniel. Drawing of Alice upsetting the jury box. By permission of the Houghton Library, Harvard University.

and (so far as he is a judge) first-rate specimens of the art of wood-engraving."[16] A decade later Carroll again commissioned the Dalziels to engrave illustrations for one of his books—the illustrations by A. B. Frost for *Rhyme? and Reason?* (1883). Apparently he was satisfied with their engravings for *Alice*.

Rossetti was harder to please. "I have . . . designed five blocks for Tennyson," he wrote to a friend in 1857, "some of which are still cutting and maiming."

It is a thankless task. After a fortnight's work my block goes to the engraver, like Agag, delicately, and is hewn to pieces before the—Lord Harry!

Address to the D——l Brothers

O woodman, spare that block,
O gash not anyhow;
It took ten days by clock,
I'd fain protect it now.

Chorus, wild laughter from Dalziel's workshop.

Rossetti once virtually acknowledged that the problem was his fault for using chalk and wash to model his drawings, instead of distinct pencil or ink lines.[17] And yet he allowed the engraver no artistic licence, despite claiming large freedom for himself as an illustrator of Tennyson's text.

However, Rossetti did distinguish between visionary poems that gave the illustrator broad artistic license, and those others—those "absolutely narrative as in the old ballads, for instance"—that he thought were so literal as to keep the artist from allegorizing on his own hook. "Are we to try the experiment ever in their regard?" he wondered, coveting for himself yet another degree of artistic freedom.[18] Ruskin more decisively liberated *all* "good pictures" from their poetic texts. His reference to the nominally "subordinate" nature of illustration, in the letter to Tennyson, was probably just a courtesy to the poet. In any case a variety of arguments can free illustration from subordination to the text.

Some illustrations have literal priority over the text that they are supposed to illustrate, because they were drawn before the text was written. If any question of subordination affects such illustrations, it is the other way round. Rowlandson's illustrations of William Combe's *Dr. Syntax* books (1812–21) were of this sort; and Charles Dickens was hired to write letterpress that would annotate plates for *The Pickwick Papers*, though in fact he very quickly seized control from the unfortunate artist, Robert Seymour. (Late in his life George Cruikshank claimed, without much justification, that Dickens wrote *Sketches by Boz* and *Oliver Twist* to complement his drawings for these works. He made similar claims for some of W. Harrison Ainsworth's novels, apparently with better cause.) The popular annual gift books of the early Victorian period could be explicit about the secondary status of the text: one such book advertised its poems and prose pieces as "being no unfit companions to the beautiful engravings which they are intended to illustrate."[19]

Even less closely related than texts "written up to" illustrations in this way are texts and illustrations that have independent origins, and that gain the appearance of shared reference only through editorial intervention. For example, in the nineteenth century it was common for Bewick's many small woodcuts to be reused to "illustrate" a variety of textual scenes. In effect they were treated as stock printer's blocks. And the same frugal use could be made of more elaborate designs. The Dalziel Brothers in particular would shamelessly "botch" things this way—so Eric de Maré has complained. He cites as examples their strikingly irrelevant reuse of a handsome block by Frederick Sandys, and similar treatment of two blocks by J. M. Whistler, all for Walter Thornbury's *Historical and Legendary Ballads and Songs* (1876).[20]

Tenniel himself did not escape such recycling: the same block that illustrated the death of the heroine Zelica in Moore's *Lalla Rookh* (1861) was used again to represent, in Thornbury's book, the death of a nameless Persian bride (fig. 11.6). No matter that in his text Moore mentioned the sol-

Fig. 11.6. Tenniel. The death of Zelica. From Thomas Moore, *Lalla Rookh* (1861).

diers standing by "with pity in their eyes," but that Thornbury did not: the Dalziels found the block as appropriate for the new text as for the old.[21]

Cruikshank's notorious claim to have originated *Sketches by Boz* and *Oliver Twist* is not usually taken seriously, but J. Hillis Miller has shown how, in the experience of the reader, it might as well be true. Cruikshank's pictures, being more obvious than the text, are likely to be read first, making the text a belated adjunct to the pictures. "Within the atemporal realm of the finished works Cruikshank's drawings seem prior, originating. They appear to be the radiant source beside which Dickens' words are secondary, from which they appear to have derived." Miller goes on to call into question ordinary assumptions about the mimetic or referential function of illustration.[22] His analysis has a bearing on the problematic aspects of illustration that were debated by Tennyson, Hunt, Rossetti, and Ruskin, and that necessarily affect the Tenniel illustrations.

On the standard assumption, as Miller describes it, text and pictures reflect the same reality—or the same fiction—so that the partial information supplied by the text can be filled out with complementary information supplied by the pictures. In the picture we are commonly supposed to be able to "see more exactly what a character or scene 'really looked like.' " On this assumption the criterion for good illustration is that the pictures give a faithful rendition of the world that the text mirrors also.

A cruder version of this assumption takes for granted the mimetic adequacy of the text, and asks of the pictures only that they faithfully mirror the text itself. For obvious reasons authors—such as Tennyson—will incline toward this view. The idea that illustration is secondary and epiphenomenal has some justification in the early history of the words *illustrate* and *illustration*. Originally these words denoted the illumination, elucidation, or enhancement of things or concepts—previously existing things or concepts.[23] And the basic, nonpictorial senses of the words remained common well into the nineteenth century; there were no pictures, for example, in Harriet Martineau's *Illustrations of Political Economy* (1832–34). When the words *illustrate* and *illustration* did get applied to pictorial illustration, they kept their flavor of secondariness. So it was not strange for Tennyson to expect illustrations to be subordinate to the text.

Miller deconstructs only the more complex of these two mimetic models, but the cruder, text-centered, Tennysonian one obviously suffers with it:

> The relation between text and illustration is clearly reciprocal. Each refers to the other. Each illustrates the other, in a continual back and forth movement which is incarnated in the experience of the reader as his eyes move from words to picture and back again, juxtaposing the two in a mutual establishment of meaning. Illustrations in a work of fiction displace the sign-referent relationship assumed in a mimetic reading and replace it by a complex and problematic reference between two radically different kinds of sign, the linguistic and the graphic. Illustrations establish a relation between elements within the work which shortcircuits the apparent reference of the literary text to some real world outside. . . . Such an intrinsic relation between text and picture sets up an oscillation or shimmering of meaning in which neither element can be said to be prior. The pictures are about the text; the text is about the pictures.[24]

Furthermore, the presupposition of such mutual reference is *difference*—a difference betwen the two kinds of sign ("linguistic" vs. "graphic"), and a consequent difference in the contents of the signs. It is impossible to say something the same way in pictures as in words; therefore, impossible to say quite the same thing. Such was the argument that Hunt made to Tennyson. What Tennyson failed to understand is that there is no question of discrepancy between text and illustration, only of difference. As Ruskin said in his letter, "Good pictures . . . are always another poem . . . *wholly different*" (emphasis added). The ultimate and surprising implication of the old axiom *traduttore, traditore* is to absolve the "translator" (whether in words or pictures) of any guilt. Some artists, like Rossetti, will gladly exploit this absolution.

Whatever the general truth of the claim that text has no priority over illustration, it seems to fit *Alice's Adventures in Wonderland* particularly well. Alice's dual requirements for a useful book—"pictures" and "conversations"—are remarkable not only for putting pictures first but also for not mentioning descriptions. Young readers are easily bored by scenic descriptions; Carroll wisely let the pictures that he commissioned from Tenniel do much of his descriptive work for him. Twice in *Alice's Adventures* Carroll refers the reader to an illustration for some descriptive detail—and thereby implies a kind of priority for the illustrations over the text. (In *The Nursery Alice*, outfitted with enlarged and colored pictures to make up for a greatly reduced text, Carroll often interrupts his story to discuss the pictures.) Furthermore, as Richard Kelly has pointed out in a recent essay, the physical appearances of the major characters of *Alice's Adventures* can hardly be guessed from what Carroll says in the text: to visualize clearly how most of them look, the reader must first look at the pictures.[25] Much the same is true of *Through the Looking-Glass*. And of course the text of *Through the Looking-Glass* was written under the influence of the earlier illustrations to *Alice's Adventures*, especially as regards the continuing character and image of Alice.

Granting that Carroll's text and Tenniel's pictures are virtually simultaneous and "about" each other, and also that such mutual reference presupposes not identity but difference, in what general ways does the basic difference reveal itself? And what is the reader to make of any particular difference?

Most generally, and least subtly, illustrations will differ from the text in the matter of narrative emphasis. Even when the scene of the illustration corresponds directly to a specific scene in the narrative—which is usually the case for both Carroll's own illustrations to *Alice* and Tenniel's—the illustration, as an illustration, is foregrounded, and therefore more emphatic than the corresponding passage by itself. By italicizing the passage, so to speak, the illustration heightens it, and distinguishes the whole narrative from what it would be without the illustration. That is why what Hodnett calls "the moment of choice" is so important.[26] Carroll, who knew this, probably chose *which* narrative moments Tenniel was to illustrate, so as to control, himself, the novelties of emphasis that illustrations inevitably bring about.

At the same time, he saw to it that the "point of view" of the illustrations faithfully matched the corresponding point of view of the narration. The omniscient third-person narrator who tells the story of Alice in each book varies his attention from scenes in which Alice is an important protagonist and the main object of our observation, to scenes in which she figures mainly as an observer, and in which the narration foregrounds the things that Alice sees. Tenniel varies his pictorial point of view in a similar way. The contrast of the trial scene (fig. 3.1) and the garden scene (fig. 6.1)—otherwise alike in many details—shows the use of such rhetorical variation. The trial scene is a remarkable scene in itself, something that holds Alice's attention and ours, without Alice's participation. But the power of the garden scene, as narrated and as shown in the illustration, lies in the threat that it poses to Alice—who properly plays a leading role in the narration and in the picture. (Alice appears and disappears like this in Carroll's own illustrations—for example,

figures 6.4 and 3.2.) In this respect Tenniel's illustrations "differ" from the text less than do those that Barry Moser produced for the recent and remarkable Pennyroyal Edition of *Alice's Adventures*, where all the illustrations between Alice's falling asleep and her waking leave Alice herself literally out of the picture.[27]

Given a narrative scene underscored by a corresponding illustration, typically in the same rhetorical mode, several other kinds of difference might be involved. These can be classed roughly as differences of style and differences of content—not a subtle or precise distinction (the matter of point of view, for example, straddles it), but one that does capture a habit of Victorian comment on illustration. The dispute between Tennyson and Hunt about the Lady of Shalott is typical in focusing on matters of content, not style—in part because it is hard to be articulate about visual nuance. Most of the paragraphs that follow consider, in Victorian fashion, differences of content between text and illustration; but some stylistic differences also call for comment.

Of course the most general aspect of the "style" of the Tenniel illustrations has less to do with Tenniel than with the medium in which he worked, black-and-white wood engraving. The general impression made by the *Alice* illustrations would be quite different if they were chromolithographs, or even hand-colored black-and-white engravings—two other Victorian options. Economics and the sixties vogue for "black-and-white" together determined Carroll's choice of technology, which had its consequences.

As a series of visions in black and white, the Tenniel illustrations inevitably differ from the sometimes colorful details of Alice's dreams. The red chessmen, the red paint on the white roses, the green hedges of the checkerboard landscape, the golden key and the golden crown: Tenniel reduces all of these to combinations of black and white.

And yet the reduction is not a major loss, for color does not saturate Alice's dreams. Scenes are more likely to be "bright" or "dark" than specifically colored. Alice sees "the bright flower-beds and the cool fountains"; or, finding herself in "a little dark shop," she is attracted to "a large bright thing, that looked sometimes like a doll and sometimes like a work-box." In *Alice's Adventures* the Caterpillar may be "blue," the King's crown may rest on "a crimson velvet cushion," and the Queen may turn "crimson with fury," but there are not many other striking details of color in either book. Even "the little golden key"—a much-repeated phrase—is more a nominal formula than a vivid perception; and the red chessmen are easily imagined as their conventional black equivalents—significant because not white. (The Red Queen herself is a transformation of a black kitten.) Carroll's hobby as a photographer may have something to do with the understatement of color in the two books.

If Tenniel's illustrations were brightly colored they would differ more than they now do from Carroll's narrative style, which usually avoids particularizing, and is more conceptual than visual. Of the several later efforts that *have* been made to color the Tenniel illustrations, the most successful one, by Fritz Kredel, uses the least color.[28]

Despite the fact that wood engraving suppresses color, it of course accommodates a large variety of artistic styles. The several John Leech engravings that have already been cited are sufficiently close to Tenniel's work historically and stylistically to throw some of Tenniel's traits into relief.[29] Leech's line is more casual and calligraphic; by contrast Tenniel's mature style can seem precise, literal-minded, "wooden" (as it has sometimes been called). Even the strain of youthful caricature that survives in Tenniel's *Alice* drawings—most apparent in the supernumeraries, like Father William and his son (fig. 1.39) or the messenger (fig. 1.14)—has been domesticated into a kind of literal explicitness. Tenniel may have prided himself on not using any models, but his image of the Gryphon looks as if it were drawn from the life.

The straightforward sobriety of the Tenniel illustrations befits Carroll's deadpan narration of Alice's adventures. What is wonderful about Wonderland is not that the dream is fantastic but that it feels real; and the pictures convey this matter-of-fact actuality as effectively as the text. By contrast, Carroll's own illustrations show the quirkiness of an incredible homemade world.

The Tenniel illustrations differ in content from Carroll's narrative as modestly as they differ in style. Hardly any of the differences involve positive *contradiction* of the text. Most involve either *supplementation* (the addition of details not specified in the text), or *neglect* (the omission of textual details that might be expected to appear within the picture frame), or *selection* (the omission of some textual details by leaving them outside the picture frame).[30]

Tenniel's Duchess exemplifies both contradiction and supplementation. It is a contradiction of the text (noticed by Richard Kelly) for Tenniel to show the Duchess as having a broad and bulky chin: Carroll three times describes it as a "sharp little chin"—one that Alice doesn't want to have pressed onto her shoulder. But Tenniel's rendering of the Duchess's headdress goes beyond or supplements what the text specifies. Indeed, no matter how Tenniel had shown the top of the Duchess's head, he could not have avoided going beyond the description in the text—which is nil. George Somes Layard made this general point in his late Victorian essay on the Moxon illustrated Tennyson. He shared Tennyson's dislike of any illustrator's coming "into direct collision with his author," but believed that it was

> quite another thing for the artist to import into his work particulars that have been ignored in, but are not inconsistent with, the author's production. Indeed, when we consider the matter closely, it is inevitable throughout that this should be the case. To take an obvious example, Tennyson does not even mention the Lady of Shalott's hair; but that would hardly preclude Mr. Hunt from representing her other than bald.[31]

By the same token, Tenniel had to picture the Duchess's head in *some* way not specifically authorized by the text.

Nonetheless, though supplementation is necessary to illustration, it will be more or less remarkable depending upon how well it jibes with the reader's expectations. Tenniel's basic image of Alice supplements what the text specifies, but it would not have been remarkable for Victorian readers, because it conformed so much to the expected type. (The type, as we have seen, was familiar to Tenniel; and it is not special to him. See, for example, figure 11.7, a characteristic cartoon by Leech; *Punch*, 27 February 1864.) The supplementary image of the Duchess, however, is quite remarkable: the reader would have had no reason to expect such grotesquely disproportionate features in a Duchess, even an "ugly" one, nor any outsized headdress, nor indeed any medieval headdress at all. By being unexpected the supplementary image calls attention to itself and raises the question of motivation. Perhaps, as we have already considered, the image of the Duchess refers to the iconographic tradition of the supposedly hideous duchess Margaret Maultasche. The reference may have been Carroll's idea; or possibly Tenniel was allegorizing on his own hook, greatly elaborating the sole mention of the Duchess as "ugly." (Of course the contemporary audience for such a recherché reference would not have been very large; it verges on a private joke. But private jokes do occur in these two books.)

The work of this image as a supplement to the text is more typical than is its work as a contradiction. For aside from the blunt chin that Tenniel gave the Duchess, there are virtually

Grandpapa. "HEYDAY! WHAT MAKES MY LITTLE DARLING SO CROSS?"
Little Darling. "WHY, GRANDPA, MAMMA WANTS ME TO GO TO A PANTOMIME IN THE DAY TIME, AS IF I WAS A MERE CHILD!"

Fig. 11.7. John Leech. "Little Darling." From *Punch*, 27 February 1864.

no contradictory images in the *Alice* books.[32] There is, however, another kind of contradiction to acknowledge, not contradiction of the text, but contradiction of another illustration as regards some aspect not mentioned in the text: iconic inconsistency. For example, the White Rabbit, on his first appearance, wears a solid-colored waistcoat; but two chapters later, as he crashes into the cucumber-frame, the waistcoat matches his checked jacket. There are several ways to explain this: the Rabbit changed his waistcoat; Alice changed her dream; Tenniel or Dalziel forgot what the Rabbit was wearing. Similar accounts might explain why the Mad Hatter's bow tie points to the left in three illustrations but to the right in one—or there may just have been some mixup in

imposing Tenniel's drawing onto the woodblock, which reverses left/right relationships. Tweedledum's tie even changes style between figures 1.1 and 1.3.

The frontispiece to *Alice's Adventures* (fig. 3.1) diverges from the text in a way that might seem contradictory of the text but that is in fact more a matter of selection than of contradiction. Carroll sets the scene for the trial by mentioning "a great crowd assembled about" the King and Queen— "all sorts of little birds and beasts, as well as the whole pack of cards." Tenniel omits most of this from his frontispiece, selecting only the central details; but the reader can imagine the crowd as extending beyond the picture frame.

In fact, Tenniel will often be extremely selective, de-emphasizing background and setting altogether, focusing instead on one or two characters. Anne Clark has suggested that this close visual focus matches Carroll's narrative interest: "Both author and illustrator were concerned primarily with characters, and very little with setting. Tenniel's background is rarely more than a little cross-hatching."[33] It is true that many of the vignettes are like that: what we see is a character or two at a significant moment of action, with most other details omitted (for example, figures 1.14, 1.20, and 3.3). But Tenniel also drew some fully developed backgrounds—which usually show a good deal more than the narrative specifies. He was likely to enlarge his focus to take into account a distinctive landscape setting (for example, figures 1.37, 1.39, 6.1), but he could also provide fully detailed genre interiors (for example, the two interiors in the "Father William" series; the scene of Alice and the Sheep in the shop). Most of the illustrations have a moderately close focus, showing enough background detail to anchor the scene (for example, figures 5.1, 7.1, 8.2, 9.1).

Not all omissions can be explained as a matter of selective close focus; some result from mere neglect. For example, the jug of milk that the March Hare upsets at the tea-party doesn't show in figure 5.1: it should be there, close to the March Hare and the Dormouse (while moving to take the Dormouse's place, the March Hare "upset the milk-jug into his plate")—not offstage, at the imaginable other end of the table.[34] In most cases, like this one, the detail (usually a minor detail) gets mentioned only several pages away from the narrative moment that the picture illustrates; no wonder that Tenniel and Carroll overlooked it. Even Homer nods.

The frontispiece to *Looking-Glass* (fig. 7.1) is harder to "place" in its narrative than the frontispiece to *Alice's Adven-*

tures, so its fidelity is harder to judge. There is a passage of high sentiment in chapter 8, which frames the moment when the White Knight sings "A-sitting On A Gate," to a tune of his own invention:

> Years afterwards she could bring the whole scene back again, as if it had been only yesterday—the mild blue eyes and kindly smile of the Knight—the setting sun gleaming through his hair, and shining on his armour in a blaze of light that quite dazzled her—the horse quietly moving about, with the reins hanging loose on his neck, cropping the grass at her feet—and the black shadows of the forest behind—all this she took in like a picture, as, with one hand shading her eyes, she leant against a tree, watching the strange pair, and listening, in a half dream, to the melancholy music of the song.

"Like a picture," but not quite like *this* picture; for though the sunlight and shadows are there, Alice is not shading her eyes, not leaning against any tree, and the White Knight is not singing, and the horse is not free to crop grass.

But there is no contradiction if the picture shows a different moment in the story, one close to the moment described above but not explicitly mentioned in the text; this would be a fairly ordinary supplementation. Or the picture may show a later moment that *is* mentioned in the text, the important moment when Alice and the Knight part, soon after the end of his song:

> As the Knight sang the last words of the ballad, he gathered up the reins, and turned his horse's head along the road by which they had come. "You've only a few yards to go," he said, "down the hill and over that little brook, and then you'll be a Queen—But you'll stay and see me off first?" he added as Alice turned with an eager look in the direction to which he pointed. "I shan't be long. You'll wait and wave your handkerchief when I get to that turn in the road? I think it'll encourage me, you see."
>
> "Of course I'll wait," said Alice: "and thank you very much for coming so far—and for the song—I liked it very much."
>
> "I hope so," the Knight said doubtfully: "but you didn't cry so much as I thought you would."
>
> So they shook hands, *and then the Knight rode slowly away into the forest.* [Emphasis added.]

On this reading, what the frontispiece shows at the start of *Looking-Glass* is the end of the relationship between Alice and the White Knight—that is, between Alice and Lewis Carroll—just before Alice grows up and becomes a Queen. Carroll thought this image less threatening than Tenniel's drawing of the Jabberwock, which it displaced from the front of the book, but it represents an equivalent crisis.

There is, as we have seen, one strikingly contradictory aspect of the frontispiece: the White Knight's advanced age. However, what that detail contradicts is not what the text says but rather Carroll's conception of the story, communicated privately to Tenniel, which is something else again.

Although in the last analysis neither frontispiece really contradicts the text, both do contain supplementary imagery that is remarkable and calls for interpretation. The bewigged eagle and parrot of figure 3.1 probably convey legal satire as well as refer to Alice Liddell's sisters, Edith and Lorina. The White Rabbit's miniscule trumpet may parody Carroll's inept drawing. Most important of all these details is the Knave's red nose, which by implication goes well beyond the confused findings of the trial to establish the Knave's guilt.

Such implication depends, of course, on information in the text (here the fact that the tarts were made "mostly" of pepper); by presupposing this textual information, the supplementary detail in effect refers to it. The reference in this frontispiece is subtle but important. The other frontispiece contains a more elaborate kind of referential supplement. Most of the paraphernalia that Tenniel loads onto the White Knight's horse is mentioned at some point during the eighth chapter, but some of it is not: the turnips; the bottle of wine hung upside down from the saddle; the wooden sword; the bell strapped to the horse's forehead. It is true that the turnips go with the carrots that Carroll *does* mention; and a wooden sword suits the childish and inept Knight; but there is more to the supplements than that. Janis Lull has shown, in a remarkable essay, that every item of the White Knight's equipment refers by synecdoche to past or future events in the story. For example, the fire irons hanging from the horse's saddle, mentioned by Carroll, refer to the White Knight's arrival in chapter 1, sliding down the fire poker; and the dangling bell, not mentioned, refers to the doorbell that Alice, as Queen Alice, will ring at the end of the book. The wooden sword is the sword that Tweedledum used in chapter 4. (Tweedledee's makeshift sword, a furled umbrella, is on the other side of the horse, not visible in the frontispiece, but conspicuous as a supplement to the text in figure 11.8.) And the bottle of wine prefigures the banquet of chapter 9. The *Looking-Glass* frontispiece, that is, is a synoptic mirror of the whole book, an emblem of the looking-glass world. And the supplementary details that Tenniel has added to this scene refer to the text just as much as do the images that the passage calls for. Carroll presumably intended the accessories that he does mention to function synoptically. It is hard to say whether the additional details, equally significant, were Tenniel's idea (his elaborating on

Fig. 11.8. Tenniel. Alice and the White Knight's horse. From *Through the Looking-Glass.*

Carroll's basic conceit) or details that Carroll called for outside the text.[35]

Not all supplementary details signify, however; some bear no special relation to the text. The unmentioned ivy that flourishes throughout the pictures of the two books carries no interpretative value. Neither does the clump of foxglove that looms behind Alice and the pig-baby, and that grows next to the Cheshire Cat's tree (figs. 11.9, 1.12). Carroll himself felt that the foxglove in the illustrations called out for

Fig. 11.9. Tenniel. Alice and the pig-baby. From *Alice's Adventures in Wonderland.*

interpretation: in *The Nursery Alice* he made it the subject of "a little lesson" in etymology. He claimed, erroneously, that the "fox" derived from "folk's," meaning "fairies'." Pharmacology may seem to offer a better ground for interpretation: foxglove is the source of digitalis, a lethal poison and, in the early nineteenth century, something of a panacea, prescribed at times even for madness. But for Tenniel foxglove is just an ordinary plant in the European landscape; it gives a decorative touch to three of his landscape drawings for *Aesop's Fables,* drawn decades earlier (for example, figure 11.10). In their insignificance both the fox-

Fig. 11.10. Tenniel. "The Fox and the Stork." From *Aesop's Fables* (1848).

glove and ivy differ from the conventionally emblematic straw on the March Hare's head, which adds to the words of the text to enforce their meaning.

Tenniel adds a detail to his picture of Humpty Dumpty which, unlike the straw, is not conventionally emblematic, but which has the same effect of reinforcing the text: the pointed coping on top of the wall, conspicuously shown in cross-section to the right of the picture (fig. 8.3). This detail is not mentioned in Carroll's text, nor the nursery rhyme; by introducing it, Tenniel magnifies the danger of Humpty's position.

Some supplementary details are equivocal. The haberdashery that Tenniel gave the Jabberwock may underline the mock-heroic tone of "Jabberwocky," or it may mitigate too much the terrible nature of the beast. And what of the clothes that Tenniel gave to the terrible Queen of Hearts? Do they make her even more terrible, as the Queen of Spades? Or do they merely give a useful pattern to the picture? The careful variation of the roundedness of the characters in the garden scene seems a clearly significant supplement to the text, but what of the ideal dome in the background?

At least it is safe to say that Tenniel's Queen of Hearts does *not* symbolize Queen Gertrude, despite the resemblance; neither does the White Queen in *Through the Looking-Glass* signify the Pope; nor the Cheshire Cat, Abraham Lincoln. Although as a political cartoonist Tenniel was an allegorist by profession, as an illustrator he did not "allegorize on his own hook" (to give a literal twist to Rossetti's figurative phrase). Most of the prototype figures discussed in the earlier chapters are prototypes only, not symbolic referents. In general Tenniel operates more like Hunt than Rossetti, gamely trying to provide an equivalent in his own graphic language for a text necessarily different.

The normal metaphor for the process of illustration, which is the mimetic metaphor of the mirror, may seem especially appropriate for the *Alice* books in all their many symmetries; but the metaphor is flawed, like the mirror itself. Imitation always drifts and differs—a truism as old as Plato. It follows that no illustration can simply "reflect" a text. But it does not follow that text and illustration are fundamentally at odds. Though an illustration cannot copy a text, it can—indeed, as an illustration it must—recreate part of the same world that the text creates.

It has been said that Lewis Carroll liked only a single one of Tenniel's illustrations, the well-known picture of Humpty Dumpty.[36] The story is not convincing; why, if he was so disappointed, did Carroll ask Tenniel to illustrate the second book? But Tenniel's image of Humpty Dumpty, implausibly steadying himself between the impossible backward fall into mere copy and the inevitable forward fall into mere difference, is a happy emblem for the dangerous poise of his creator.

CHAPTER TWELVE

Coordinating Text and Illustration

It is notorious that Lewis Carroll was finicky about the printing of his books. He acknowledged having

> inflicted on that most patient and painstaking firm, Messrs. Macmillan and Co., about as much wear and worry as ever publishers have lived through. The day when they undertake a book for me is a *dies nefastus* for them. From that day till the book is out—an interval of some two or three years on an average—there is no pause in "the pelting of the pitiless storm" of directions and questions on every conceivable detail.[1]

For a rounded appreciation of the phrase "every conceivable detail," we will have to wait for the publication of Carroll's correspondence with the house of Macmillan, now being edited by Morton N. Cohen.[2] But there is one detailed aspect of the printing of the *Alice* books that by and large can be judged directly from the evidence of the books themselves. That aspect is the placement of the illustrations on the page, the physical relation of the illustrations to the text.

It appears that Carroll, Tenniel, and Macmillan designed the early editions of *Alice's Adventures* and *Through the Looking-Glass* so that the text and illustrations would be significantly juxtaposed on the page. Typically, textual references stand next to their pictorial referents, and the narrative moments of text and illustration are visually synchronized. In selected later editions, care was taken to preserve such significant juxtapositions. But for some other, cheaper editions, Macmillan allowed the text and illustrations to drift apart. And most modern editions show too little concern for this aspect of the *Alice* books, which greatly contributed to their distinction as illustrated books. The unusually complementary relationship of Tenniel's illustrations to Carroll's text has often been remarked. But the strength of that relationship cannot be fully appreciated in casually laid-out editions. To see how fully the Tenniel illustrations are responsive to Carroll's text, it is necessary to see them as they were originally presented on the page.

The important illustration of Alice confronting the Queen of Hearts in the garden is a good case in point (fig. 6.1). The strongly expressive postures of the Queen and Alice suggest that the drawing captures a specific moment in the dialogue. But readers of recent editions of *Alice's Adventures* might well wonder *which* moment is being illustrated; any of several highly charged moments in the scene might seem to apply. Discussing the *Alice* books with college students, I have found that they are easily misled by the layouts of modern editions.

A reader of the Oxford English Novels edition might connect Tenniel's picture to the following passage, which appears below it there:

> . . . she stood where she was, and waited.
> When the procession came opposite to Alice, they all stopped and looked at her, and the Queen said, severely, 'Who is this?' She said it to the Knave of Hearts, who only bowed and smiled in reply.
> 'Idiot!' said the Queen, tossing her head impatiently; and, turning to Alice, she went on: 'What's your name, child?'
> 'My name is Alice, so please your Majesty,' said Alice . . .[3]

A reader of either the Modern Library edition of Carroll's *Complete Works,* or of the *Annotated Alice*, might concentrate on the Queen's gesture of pointing, described in those books not far below the illustration: " 'And who are *these?*' said the Queen, pointing to the three gardeners who were lying round the rose-tree . . . they were lying on their faces, and the pattern on their backs was the same as the rest of the pack."[4] (These three cards can be seen in the lower right-hand corner of the illustration.) But a reader of the Puffin edition could too easily connect the Queen's obvious shouting in the picture to the command that is quoted immediately below it: " 'Leave off that!' screamed the Queen."[5]

For all such readers, Tenniel's illustration would carry less force than it would for a reader of the first edition, published late in 1865 (with the date "1866" on the title page). That reader would find the picture underwritten by a single sentence of the text, which doubles as a precise caption to the illustration: "The Queen turned crimson with fury, and, after glaring at her for a moment like a wild beast, began screaming, 'Off with her head! Off—' " See figure 12.1.[6] Clearly this passage best explains the Queen's demeanor.

That the original arrangement is the best arrangement

The Queen turned crimson with fury, and, after glaring at her for a moment like a wild beast, began screaming, "Off with her head! Off—"

Fig. 12.1. Page 117 of the first edition (1866) of *Alice's Adventures in Wonderland*. By permission of the Houghton Library, Harvard University.

finds support, in this case, in some external evidence. A preliminary list in Carroll's hand of all the illustrations to *Alice's Adventures* refers to each illustration in a short phrase sufficient to distinguish it from all the others; for example, "Rabbit & watch," "cucumber frame," "caterpillar," "Duchess & Alice." Carroll refers to this particular illustration as "Queen of Hearts," and then adds a line in somewhat smaller script, "(off with her head)."[7] Whether this addition was meant to clarify matters for himself or for the printer, it is clear that Carroll understood the illustration to refer to this

particular passage of the text. When he first commissioned the drawings he may have told Tenniel to illustrate this particular moment. In any case Carroll's memorandum shows that the layout of the 1866 edition reflects his sense of the illustration better than any of the modern layouts cited above.

Of course, the passage that served as a caption in 1866 describes the Queen's behavior only. To appreciate the way that Tenniel has drawn Alice here—head cocked upward in mild defiance and arms protectively crossed in front, boldly standing her ground—the reader can recall what he has just read at the bottom of the opposite page, when Alice repulsed the Queen's inquiry into the identity of the gardeners:

> "And who are *these*?" said the Queen, pointing to the three gardeners who were lying round the rose-tree . . . .
> "How should *I* know?" said Alice, surprised at her own courage. "It's no business of *mine*."

Alice's defensive posture in the illustration persists from this moment in the dialogue. The illustration is bracketed by passages that together specify the demeanor of the main characters.

The same kind of precise bracketing by the text informs Tenniel's famous illustration of the Wonderland tea party. After the Hatter has remarked to Alice, "Your hair wants cutting" (a milder version of the Queen's threat of execution), there is this brief passage at the foot of page 96: " 'You should learn not to make personal remarks,' Alice said with some severity: 'it's very rude.' " The reader next sees, at the top of the opposite page, the tea-party illustration: there Alice is still glowering at the Hatter, her left hand gripping the arm of her chair. And then, immediately below the illustration: "The Hatter opened his eyes very wide on hearing this; but all he *said* was, 'Why is a raven like a writing-desk?' " (fig. 12.2). Apparently the illustration depicts the precise moment when, wide-eyed, the Hatter put his famous riddle to Alice.

But that implication is lost in some later editions, including one published with Carroll's approval. In 1887 Macmillan published a "People's Edition" of *Alice's Adventures*, along with one of *Through the Looking-Glass*. These books were less than half the price of the standard editions, and were less luxurious: plain edges rather than gilt, no gilt ornamentation on the covers, thinner paper, and fewer pages. To reduce the number of pages it was necessary to reset the type; and inevitably that resetting disturbed the careful arrangement of text and illustrations that had been worked out for the origi-

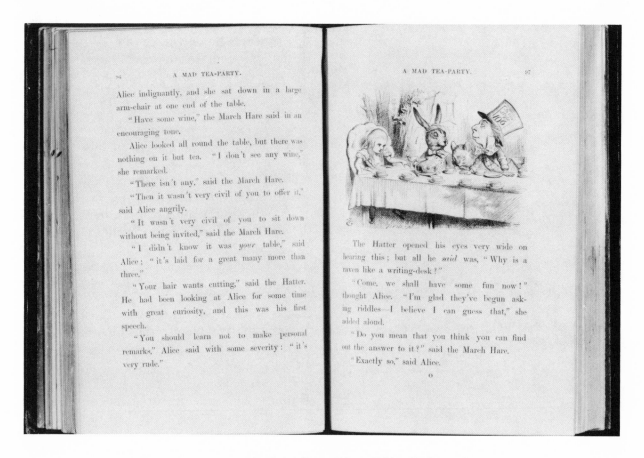

Fig. 12.2. Pages 96–97 of the first edition (1866) of *Alice's Adventures in Wonderland*. By permission of the Houghton Library, Harvard University.

nal editions. One result was the juxtaposition of the tea-party illustration with:

> "Do you mean that you think you can find out the answer to it [i.e., the riddle]?" said the March Hare.
> "Exactly so," said Alice.
> "Then you should say what you mean," the March Hare went on.[8]

Such an arrangement weakens the immediate relationship of picture to text. That relationship is further weakened in the even cheaper "Sixpenny Series" edition that Macmillan published in 1898, less than a year after Carroll's death. There the illustration is delayed until the riddle topic has lapsed from the conversation and then revived. It comes in the middle of, and seems to illustrate, this paragraph:

> Alice sighed wearily. "I think you might do something [*illustration here*] better with the time," she said, "than wasting it in asking riddles that have no answers."[9]

This arrangement ascribes "weariness" to the Alice of the illustration, where the original arrangement ascribed a certain "severity." Only in the original arrangement does the text accurately represent the picture. Or, rather, only in the original arrangement does the picture actually represent the text.

In the Norton Critical Edition of *Alice*, this drawing has floated free of any mooring in the text, and appears at the very head of the chapter, as a kind of résumé of the whole rather than as an illustration of any specific moment. The reader is denied any clue to its dramatic immediacy. The same arrangement, and the same defect, are to be found in the handsome edition of *Alice's Adventures* designed by George Salter with the Tenniel illustrations colored by Fritz Kredel, which achieved a wide distribution after World War II.[10]

Page layout matters too in the sequel, *Through the Looking-Glass*. When Alice encounters Tweedledum and Tweedledee, Tenniel shows her in an awkward, startled posture because she has just been described in the text as "startled,"

startled by a voice coming from the one marked 'DUM.'

[*the illustration appears here*]

"If you think we're wax-works," he said, "you ought to pay, you know. Wax-works weren't made to be looked at for nothing. Nohow!"

This arrangement, set out by the original edition (1872), can be seen in figure 12.3.[11] The drawing specifically shows Alice's startled response to Tweedledum's behavior. (Realistically, perhaps, Tenniel should have shown Tweedledum as

in the course of speaking; but it was preferable to show him closemouthed, the same as his twin brother—perhaps between sentences.) In later editions this illustration too drifts away from its locality. It is delayed for two pages in the Sixpenny Series edition, and ascends to the top of the chapter in both the Oxford English Novels and Puffin editions, where it illustrates the general title of the chapter, "Tweedledum and Tweedledee," but where Alice's odd posture loses its motivation.

Many other full-width illustrations in both books show to best advantage in their original settings, with the immediately relevant passage of text strategically placed as a

TWEEDLEDUM AND TWEEDLEDEE.   67

CHAPTER IV.

TWEEDLEDUM AND TWEEDLEDEE.

THEY were standing under a tree, each with an arm round the other's neck, and Alice knew which was which in a moment, because one of them had 'DUM' embroidered on his collar, and the other 'DEE.' "I suppose they've each got 'TWEEDLE' round at the back of the collar," she said to herself.

They stood so still that she quite forgot they were alive, and she was just looking round to see if the word 'TWEEDLE' was written at the back of each collar, when she was startled by a voice coming from the one marked 'DUM.'

" If you think we're wax-works," he said, "you ought to pay, you know. Wax-works weren't made to be looked at for nothing. Nohow!"

"Contrariwise," added the one marked 'DEE.' "if you think we're alive, you ought to speak."

"I'm sure I'm very sorry," was all Alice could say; for the words of the old song kept ringing through her head like the ticking of a clock, and she could hardly help saying them out loud :—

F 2

Fig. 12.3. Pages 66–67 of the first edition (1872) of *Through the Looking-Glass*.

Then they all crowded round her once more, while the Dodo solemnly presented the thimble, saying, "We beg your acceptance of this elegant thimble;" and, when it had finished this short speech, they all cheered.

Fig. 12.4. Page 35 of the first edition (1866) of *Alice's Adventures in Wonderland*. By permission of the Houghton Library, Harvard University.

caption; for example, Alice and the Dodo (fig. 12.4), or Alice dragging the White Knight out of the ditch (fig. 12.5).

Rarely in the original settings does any illustration, large or small, seem to have been displaced from its proper location without some good typographical reason. But it may be that an error was made (and overlooked by Carroll) in placing the picture that shows Alice and the two remonstrating Queens

afraid that he really *was* hurt this time. However, though she could see nothing but the soles of his feet, she was much relieved to hear that he was talking on in his usual tone. "All kinds of fastness," he repeated : "but it was careless of him to put another man's helmet on——with the man in it, too."

"How *can* you go on talking so quietly, head downwards?" Alice asked, as she dragged him out by the feet, and laid him in a heap on the bank.

Fig. 12.5. Page 172 of the first edition (1872) of *Through the Looking-Glass*.

190   QUEEN ALICE.

" I suppose——" Alice was beginning, but the Red Queen answered for her. " Bread-and-butter, of course.   Try another Subtraction sum.   Take a bone from a dog: what remains ? "

Alice considered.   " The bone wouldn't remain, of course, if I took it——and the dog wouldn't remain; it would come to bite me—— and I'm sure *I* shouldn't remain ! "

" Then you think nothing would remain ? " said the Red Queen.

" I think that 's the answer."

QUEEN ALICE.   191

" Wrong, as usual," said the Red Queen : " the dog's temper would remain."

" But I don't see how——"

" Why, look here ! " the Red Queen cried. " The dog would lose its temper, wouldn't it ? "

" Perhaps it would," Alice replied cautiously.

" Then if the dog went away, its temper would remain ! " the Queen exclaimed triumphantly.

Alice said, as gravely as she could, " They might go different ways."   But she couldn't help thinking to herself, " What dreadful nonsense we *are* talking ! "

" She can't do sums a *bit* ! " the Queens said together, with great emphasis.

" Can *you* do sums ? " Alice said, turning suddenly on the White Queen, for she didn't like being found fault with so much.

The Queen gasped and shut her eyes.   " I can do Addition," she said, " if you give me time——but I can't do Substraction, under *any* circumstances ! "

Fig. 12.6. Pages 190–91 of the first edition (1872) of *Through the Looking- Glass*.

(fig. 12.6). The simultaneous gestures of the Queens, and Alice's withdrawn appearance, suggest that this illustration belongs on the opposite page, just below the thirteenth line, " 'we *are* talking!' " No typographical constraint would prevent such an arrangement, which by bracketing the picture with two relevant sentences might better define the moment that Tenniel was illustrating.

In his list of the illustrations to *Alice's Adventures*, Carroll distinguishes between the broader illustrations meant to be centered on the page (marked κ on the list), and the narrower ones meant to be "let in," or run flush to the margin, set alongside a narrowed column of the continuing text (marked λ on the list). In some cases Carroll even specified from which margin, left or right, the illustration was to be let in. The early editions place many of these let-in illustrations precisely next to the relevant passage in the text. So the references to "a low curtain she had not noticed before, and behind it . . . a little door about fifteen inches high," occur immediately next to the illustration of these things, indeed in the same vertical sequence (fig. 12.7). So tall Alice's interjection, "Oh, my poor little feet," occurs at the very foot of the page, directly next to her distant feet (fig. 12.8; note too how Alice's height is enhanced by her vertically filling the page).

8   DOWN THE

doors of the hall ; but, alas ! either the locks were too large, or the key was too small, but at any rate it would not open any of them. However, on the second time round, she came

upon a low curtain she had not noticed before, and behind it was a little door about fifteen inches high : she tried the little golden key in the

lock, and to her great delight it fitted !

Alice opened the door and found that it led into a small passage, not much larger than a rat-hole : she knelt down and looked along the passage into the loveliest garden you ever saw. How she longed to get out of that dark hall, and wander about among those beds of bright

CHAPTER II.

THE POOL OF TEARS.

"Curiouser and curiouser!" cried Alice (she was so much surprised, that for the moment she quite forgot how to speak good English) ; "now I'm opening out like the largest telescope that ever was ! Good-bye, feet !" (for when she looked down at her feet, they seemed to be almost out of sight, they were getting so far off) "Oh, my poor little feet, I wonder

Fig. 12.7. Page 8 of the first edition (1866) of *Alice's Adventures in Wonderland*. By permission of the Houghton Library, Harvard University.

Fig. 12.8. Page 15 of the first edition (1866) of *Alice's Adventures in Wonderland*. By permission of the Houghton Library, Harvard University.

So the references to "a snatch in the air" and "a crash of broken glass" in what might be "a cucumber-frame," run in parallel with the depiction of those things (fig. 12.9). There are other examples in both books of such nice matching of marginal illustrations with the text. This finesse suffers more or less in later editions.

waiting till she fancied she heard the Rabbit just under the window, she suddenly spread out her hand, and made a snatch in the air. She did not get hold of anything, but she heard a little shriek and a fall, and a crash of broken glass, from which she concluded that it was just possible it had fallen into a cucumber-frame, or something of the sort.

Next came an angry voice—the Rabbit's— "Pat! Pat! Where are you?" And then a voice she had never heard before, "Sure then I'm here! Digging for apples, yer honour!"

"Digging for apples, indeed!" said the Rabbit angrily. "Here! Come and help me out of *this!*" (Sounds of more broken glass.)

Fig. 12.9. Page 48 of the first edition (1866) of *Alice's Adventures in Wonderland*, By permission of the Houghton Library, Harvard University.

Tenniel seems to have modeled the illustrations in figures 12.7–12.9, like several of his other illustrations for *Alice's Adventures*, on drawings that Carroll had himself sketched into the gift manuscript for Alice Liddell (see chapter 2). Of the thirty-seven drawings in that manuscript, fourteen are full-page "plates," so to speak, each one opposite the relevant page of text (most of them sideways—an awkward arrange-

ment); and twenty-three are let-in, marginal illustrations. None is centered on a page of text, though many of Tenniel's were to be later. Conversely, Tenniel designed few full-page illustrations—vertical ones—and those only for special purposes. (Two are the frontispieces; and a third, the "Jabberwocky" illustration, had originally been intended for a frontispiece. The remaining two, which show the Red Queen being shaken back into Dinah the cat, are actually small drawings, though displayed alone on the page; and they mark an important transitional moment in the *Looking-Glass* narrative.)

It is true that, because of the quantity of full-page "plates," Carroll's manuscript is less closely integrated than either of the published *Alice* books. Nonetheless, the manuscript set an important precedent for the treatment of the smaller illustrations. With only one exception, all the let-in illustrations in the manuscript stand next to the passages that they illustrate. Figure 12.10, which includes the prototype of Tenniel's drawing in figure 12.7, is a good example.[12] Tenniel improved the illustration by adding the door mentioned in the text, but the placement of the illustration in the book simply perpetuates an integration that the manuscript had already achieved. Much the same can be said of figure 12.9 and Carroll's prototype for the illustration in it. Similar care in placement was extended to most of Tenniel's "new" let-in drawings for *Alice's Adventures* (that is, those that Carroll had not attempted himself), and to the series for *Looking-Glass*.

One special kind of let-in illustration is the L-shaped kind, in which Tenniel did some of his most memorable work; the top or base of the illustration runs the full width of the page, but the other end leaves room on one side for a quadrant of the text. (There are none like this in Carroll's manuscript.) Tenniel's L-shaped drawing of Alice talking with the Cheshire Cat, which is otherwise typical, illustrates a continuing and relatively unchanging scene rather than a particular moment, so the text in the open quadrant may not have any special relevance to the picture. But even here there may be a connection between the emphasis given to the Cat's tail in the drawing and the discussion of tail-wagging reported in the quadrant (fig. 12.11). In other cases the connection of picture to text is beyond doubt. In the L-shaped illustration of the King of Hearts, the King points out the tarts on the table in front of him. In the original edition, the textual quadrant of this illustration begins, " 'Why, there they are!' said the King triumphantly, pointing to the tarts on the table." (In his list of illustrations, Carroll referred to this one as "There they are!") In the rest of the quadrant, the King continues to read from the letter that Tenniel has put in his right hand (see fig. 12.12); compare the immediacy of this arrangement to the irrelevancy of that in the People's Edition (fig. 12.13). So in the original edition of *Looking-Glass*, Humpty Dumpty

how she was ever to get out again: suddenly she came upon a little three-legged table, all made of solid glass, there was nothing lying upon it, but a tiny golden key, and Alice's first idea was that it might belong to one of the doors of the hall, but alas! either the locks were too large, or the key too small, but at any rate it would open none of them However, on the second time round, she came to a low curtain, behind which was a door about eighteen inches high: she tried the little key in the keyhole, and it fitted! Alice opened the door, and looked down a small passage, not larger than a rat-hole, into the loveliest garden you ever saw How she longed to get out of that dark hall, and wander about among those beds of bright flowers and those cool fountains, but she could not even get her head through the doorway, "and even if my head would go through" thought poor Alice, "it would be very little use without my shoulders Oh, how I wish I could shut

Fig. 12.10. Page 6 of *Alice's Adventures under Ground* (1886).

PIG AND PEPPER.   91

"Well then," the Cat went on, "you see a dog growls when it's angry, and wags its tail when it's pleased. Now *I* growl when I'm pleased, and wag my tail when I'm angry. Therefore I'm mad."

"*I* call it purring, not growling," said Alice.

"Call it what you like," said the Cat. "Do you play croquet with the Queen to-day?"

Fig. 12.11. Page 91 of the first edition (1866) of *Alice's Adventures in Wonderland*. By permission of the Houghton Library, Harvard University.

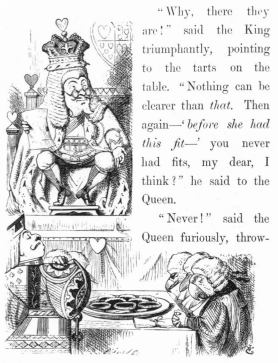

"Why, there they are!" said the King triumphantly, pointing to the tarts on the table. "Nothing can be clearer than *that*. Then again—'*before she had this fit*—' you never had fits, my dear, I think?" he said to the Queen.

"Never!" said the Queen furiously, throw-

ing an inkstand at the Lizard as she spoke. (The unfortunate little Bill had left off writing on his slate with one finger, as he found it made

using the ink, that was trickling down his face, as long as it lasted.)

"Then the words don't *fit* you," said the King, looking round the court with a smile. There was a dead silence.

"It's a pun!" the King added in an offended tone, and everybody laughed.

"Let the jury consider their verdict," the King said, for about the twentieth time that day.

Fig. 12.12. Page 186 of the first edition (1866) of *Alice's Adventures in Wonderland*. By permission of the Houghton Library, Harvard University.

Fig. 12.13. Page 169 of the People's Edition (1887) of *Alice's Adventures in Wonderland*.

and Alice join hands in both the illustrations and the textual quadrant (fig. 12.14), but not in the People's Edition.

Finally, the most remarkable example of felicitous picture placement occurs near the start of *Through the Looking-Glass*. In the original edition, the first picture of Alice passing through the mirror appears at the top of a right-hand page, captioned by the lines that describe the dissolving of the mirror and Alice's passing "through" it (fig. 12.15). Such captioning is not itself unique. But at the very moment when the text has Alice pass through the looking-glass the reader is made to turn the page, and to discover on the left what is largely a mirror-image of the illustration that he has just been looking at, now presented as a view, from the *other* side of the looking-glass, of Alice's passing through it (fig. 12.16). These two complementary images are printed on opposite sides of the same leaf, in close registration with each other. The leaf, in effect, is the glass. Even the monogram of the artist fills the same space on the different sides of the leaf; and so does the signature of the engraver. Tenniel thoughtfully reversed his monogram left-to-right, so that in the second illustration it is seen as if through the leaf. The Dalziel signature, unfortunately, defies reversal on the other side of the looking-glass; commercial interests, unlike artistic ones, resist imaginative transformation.

The People's Edition preserves the superimposition of these two illustrations on opposite sides of the same leaf, but below them the "captions" of text have drifted irrelevantly. The Norton Critical Edition recovers the intended effect remarkably well, given the different typographical requirements of the standard page in that edition. The Oxford English Novels edition, by placing these illustrations on facing pages, enables the reader to study the reflective symmetry of the two pictures; but it prevents him from experiencing with Alice the transition from one side of the looking-glass to the other.

Besides the People's Editions of the *Alice* books, to which reference has already been made, there were several other relevant editions published during Carroll's lifetime. Macmillan published translations of *Alice's Adventures* in 1869 (German and French) and 1872 (Italian). Despite the elasticity that translation imposes on a text, these books preserve much of the rapport between text and illustration that marks the original edition. There is published evidence that Carroll took a special interest in the matter; Warren Weaver's useful

118   HUMPTY DUMPTY.

fell off the wall in doing so) and offered Alice his hand. She watched him a little anxiously as she took it. "If he smiled much more, the ends of his mouth might meet behind," she thought: "and then I don't know what would happen to his head! I'm afraid it would come off!"

"Yes, all his horses and all his men," Humpty

Fig. 12.14. Page 118 of the first edition (1872) of *Through the Looking-Glass*.

study of translations of the *Alice* books quotes from some of the letters that Carroll wrote to Macmillan in 1868 regarding the German translation of *Alice's Adventures*. Two weeks after complaining about some page proofs that were each "a line too short, and one-half inch too narrow . . . [throwing] most

there.   And certainly the glass *was* beginning
to melt away, just like a bright silvery mist.

In another moment Alice was through the

Fig. 12.15. Page 11 of the first edition (1872) of *Through the Looking-Glass*.

glass, and had jumped lightly down into the
Looking-glass room.   The very first thing she did
was to look whether there was a fire in the

Fig. 12.16. Page 12 of the first edition (1872) of *Through the Looking-Glass*.

of the pictures out of proportion," Carroll spelled out a general requirement for the German edition that obviously applies as well to the layouts of both the original edition of *Alice's Adventures* and the forthcoming edition of *Looking-Glass* (as yet unwritten): "I forgot to say, with regard to the German Alice, that they need not trouble themselves to get into each page the *same* matter as is in the corresponding page in the English. Let them run it on as they like, *so long as they place the pictures as near as possible to the text to which they refer*."[13] As a result of such attention the Macmillan editions of the three translations are more accurately laid out than most modern editions of the English text.

Of at least equal interest are the so-called ninth edition of *Alice's Adventures* and the so-called fourth edition of *Looking-Glass*, both published in 1897, which, aside from the People's Editions, were the only editions of the English texts to be published in Carroll's lifetime that actually involved resetting. Except for small verbal revisions, these new editions, unlike the People's Editions, were page-for-page and line-for-line replicas of the original editions, and so they preserved the same subtleties of layout. Macmillan reprinted these editions many times, both in London and New York, at least into the 1940's.[14]

The early layouts have survived, too, in photofacsimile editions of the original editions, including some still in print. In 1941 the Book League of America published a facsimile edition of "the first edition" of *Alice's Adventures*—the edition of 1866, judging from internal evidence.[15] There was some effort to reproduce the original binding, and a general literary introduction (by Kathleen Norris) was added. The half-title page bears the signature of C. L. Dodgson, but no textual note identifies the provenance of the copy that this edition reproduces.

According to the *National Union Catalog*, Crown Publishers (New York) published a facsimile of the first edition of *Alice's Adventures* in 1957.[16] That may have been the first issue of a facsimile edition which is still in print, now bearing the imprint of Avenel Books, a division of Crown. This Avenel facsimile of the 1866 edition seems to derive from either the Book League facsimile or from the copy of the original edition that it reproduces. The same signature of C. L. Dodgson appears on the half-title, in the same location. Indeed, the same half-title, signature and all, puts in an illegitimate second appearance, just before the first chapter.

A parallel facsimile edition of *Looking-Glass*, apparently the 1872 edition, is also published by Avenel. It too is somewhat casually made up: pages 217 (devoted to Tenniel's illustration of the cat Dinah, held in Alice's hands) and 218 (the start of chapter 12), which are unnumbered sides of the same leaf, have accidentally changed places. This error persists in the combined edition of these two facsimiles that was published in 1979 by Derrydale Books, another Crown subsidiary, under the title *Journeys in Wonderland*. However, the autographed half-title has been confined to its proper location.

The foreword to this book, by Patricia Horan, is uninformative; but whoever wrote the dust-jacket copy understood in general what I have tried to specify: "This new edition is a splendid opportunity for Alice to find her way into new hands and new imaginations. These two masterpieces. . . . are reprinted here with the original text and the magnificent John Tenniel illustrations, the ones approved by Lewis Carroll himself. All ninety-two illustrations are here, *in their proper places* [emphasis added]." All, that is, except for the picture of Dinah meant for page 217.

Many of the illustrations in this modern reprint are poorly reproduced, with a loss of fine detail. Carroll's original publishers, Macmillan in London, have recently published more careful facsimile editions of both *Alice* books, which show the Tenniel illustrations to better advantage, and make clear how well Tenniel's illustrations integrate with Carroll's text.[17]

Notes

INTRODUCTION

1. Set in Africa, *The Hatchet Throwers* was conventionally imperialist and racist. Lionel Lambourne reproduces several of Griset's illustrations for the book in *Ernest Griset: Fantasies of a Victorian Illustrator* (London: Thames and Hudson, 1979), pp. 43–45; see also pp. 13, 42.

2. *Times*, 26 December 1865, p. 5.

3. The quotations from the *Pall Mall Gazette* and *Aunt Judy's Magazine* are taken from the early reviews of *Alice's Adventures* reprinted in *Jabberwocky* 9 (1979–80): 3–8, 27–39. See also Elizabeth A. Cripps, "*Alice* and the Reviewers," *Children's Literature* 11 (1983): 32–48.

The review in *Aunt Judy's Magazine* was not disinterested. The editor and presumable reviewer, Mrs. Alfred Gatty, had published a series of successful children's books called *Parables from Nature*, the third (1861) including an illustration by Tenniel; and she had been on friendly terms with Carroll in Oxford at least since the early sixties.

4. "Mr. Tenniel's Lalla Rookh," *Times*, 31 October 1860, p. 9. See also 24 December 1860, p. 10. Though dated "1861" on the title page, *Lalla Rookh* was published in time for the Christmas trade, 1860.

5. For a description of most Tenniel scholarship and criticism, see the bibliography, pp. 145–46.

6. These last two wants may soon be met, at least in part: Frankie Morris has undertaken a dissertation on the *Punch* career for the Department of Art History and Archaeology, University of Missouri—Columbia; and Justin G. Schiller is compiling a census of Tenniel's *Alice* drawings.

CHAPTER 1

1. See below, p. 27. Apparently Carroll chose Tenniel on the advice of Robinson Duckworth. A Fellow of Trinity College, Duckworth had accompanied Carroll and the three Liddell sisters on the river outing during which Carroll first improvised his story about Alice. See *The Lewis Carroll Picture Book*, ed. Stuart Dodgson Collingwood (1899; rpt. Detroit: Tower, 1971), p. 360.

2. Sarzano, p. 18. Marguerite Mespoulet, *Creators of Wonderland* (New York: Arrow Editions, 1934).

3. Phyllis Cunnington and Anne Buck, *Children's Costume in England* (London: Adam & Charles Black, 1965), pp. 172–75; Doreen Yarwood, *The Encyclopedia of World Costume* (New York: Scribners, 1978), p. 78; Elizabeth Ewing, *History of Children's Costume* (New York: Scribners, 1977), pp. 46–48, 63–64.

In chapter 6 of *Sketches by Boz* (1836), Charles Dickens meditated nostalgically on "a patched and much-soiled skeleton suit" found in a used-clothing market. It was one of those straight blue cloth cases in which small boys used to be confined, before belts and tunics had come in, and old notions had gone out: an ingenious contrivance for displaying the full symmetry of a boy's figure, by fastening him into a very tight jacket, with an ornamental row of buttons over each shoulder, and then buttoning his trousers over it, so as to give his legs the appearance of being hooked on, just under the armpits." (*Sketches by Boz*, Oxford Illustrated Dickens [1957; rpt. London: Oxford University Press, 1973], pp. 75–76.)

In 1852 Dickens added a skeleton suit "gave the wearer something of a trussed appearance, like a young fowl ready for the spit. It was a dreadful fashion, as offering irresistible temptations to the schoolmaster to use his cane." Compare Alice's magisterial response to the twins' outfits. (*Charles Dickens' Uncollected Writings from* Household Words, *1850–1859*, ed. Harry Stone, 2 vols. [Bloomington: Indiana University Press, 1968], 2:413.)

4. Spielmann, p. 471. George du Maurier, another *Punch* artist, commented that Tenniel's *Alice* illustrations "belong to the old school. . . . Perhaps we, of the new school, are too much the slaves of the model" ("The Illustrating of Books from the Serious Artist's Point of View: I," *Magazine of Art* 13 [1890]: 351).

5. Though Leech, like Tenniel, did not sign all his work, this cartoon is recognizably his.

Carroll's text specifies much of the detail in Tenniel's illustration: "things . . . such as bolsters, blankets, hearth-rugs, table-cloths, dish-covers, and coal-scuttles"; also the saucepan-helmet. Though the twins strangely enough find these things in a "wood," they are the household items that a Victorian child would most readily convert into armor for war games.

6. Figure 1.9 is from chapter 18 in the series "Punch's Book of British Costumes," which ran from 4 February to 29 December 1860. The many illustrations for the series are unsigned, but most if not all of them are by Tenniel. It is possible that he wrote some of the letterpress as well; see Spielmann, pp. 355, 372. Tenniel had made a special study of costume when an art student.

From time to time, the series cites the authority of (among others) F. W. Fairholt, who wrote *Costume in England* (London: Chapman and Hall, 1846; 2d ed., 1860). Several of the illustrations for the series are silently copied (with ironic commentary) or adapted from illustrations in Fairholt's history. Figure 1.9 obviously derives from figure 1.10, which appears on p. 159 of the first edition.

7. From about 1839 a member of the Whig party in the United States might be called a "coon" because of the raccoon emblem of the party; Lincoln had a been a Whig until the party disintegrated after the 1856 election. There may also be a racist slur implied.

Tenniel was not the sole author of his political cartoons. The basic "idea" for each cartoon was usually invented by the *Punch* editorial staff at their weekly meeting. Tenniel illustrated the ideas of others—for *Punch* as for *Alice*.

8. *The Works of James Gillray* (London: Henry G. Bohn, 1851; rpt. New York: Benjamin Blom, 1968), pl. 136. See also Mary Dorothy George, *Catalogue of Political and Personal Satires Preserved in the Department of Prints and Drawings in the British Museum*, vol. 7 (London: British Museum, 1942), pp. 198–99, no. 8684.

9. In *Creators of Wonderland*, pp. 44–45, Mespoulet compares Tenniel's drawing of the Frog-Footman to two drawings by Grandville.

Despite the caption given for it on p. 62 of *Tenniel's Alice*, Carroll's own drawing of figure 1.14 is probably not a "design" for Tenniel's drawing but a copy of it. Not mentioned in *Tenniel's Alice*—though drawn on the other half of the same sheet of paper (in the Harvard collection)—is Carroll's drawing of the Tweedledum shown in figure 1.3. On the evidence of figures 1.2 and 1.4, this juvenile character type was Tenniel's long before Carroll wrote about Tweedledum; therefore it is probable that both of these Carroll drawings were copied from the Tenniel illustrations.

10. The joke on the *Standard* and the *Morning Herald*, newspapers that were much the same because under the same management, dates back to a squib accompanied by a cartoon by Leech, published in December 1845, p. 262; see Spielmann, pp. 211–13. The crinoline was a later addition, calculated to keep Mrs. Gamp in the rear guard of fashion, and Tenniel perpetuated this detail in cartoons of Mrs. Gamp published 16 July 1864, 11 August 1866, and 22 August 1868.

In figure 1.18, "The Idle Gossips," Mrs. Gamp and Mrs. Harris are complaining of Palmerston's failing health, and looking forward to his replacement as prime minister by either Benjamin Disraeli or the earl of Derby.

11. Pius IX was made uneasy by the prospect of the French emperor, Napoleon III (right), withdrawing his forces from Italy and leaving Rome to the mercy of Victor Emmanuel II (left, trying to remove traces of Garibaldi's recent unsuccessful campaign). In this and many similar cartoons, Tenniel reduces the Pope's triple crown to a mobcap, to go with the crinoline.

12. Figure 1.22, which represents the pope as a Mohammedan, alludes to an extended controversy that involved Nicholas Wiseman and Sydney Morgan. In her travel book *Italy* (1821), Lady Morgan reported that some French antiquarians had impugned the supposed Chair of St. Peter by uncasing it and discovering on it the inscription, in Arabic, "There is but one God, and Mahomet is his prophet." Wiseman, then rector of the English College in Rome, rejected her account in a pamphlet (1833). In the general controversy that attended his elevation in 1850 to cardinal archbishop of Westminster, the topic was revived, occasioning a pamphlet by Lady Morgan that went through four editions in 1851. Figure 1.21 is Tenniel's caricature of Wiseman, sitting atop his cardinal's red hat.

13. Caption: "THE ENGLISH BEEF, THE FRENCH WINE, AND THE GERMAN SAUSAGES. / The Beef. 'Now, look here, you "small Germans," don't jump out of the frying-pan into the fire—that's all.' " The frying pan is labelled "SCHLESWIG and HOLSTEIN."

The Beef is John Bull; the bottle is Napoleon III. Bavaria and the other lesser German states (here the "small Germans"—small German sausages) were at that time resisting a scheme by Prussia and Austria that would have given nominal protection to long-standing Danish claims in the duchy of Schleswig. England here warns them of the dangers of intransigency.

14. Despite the apparent initials "EB," the flattened triangle was Frank Bellew's hallmark; see Spielmann, pp. 500–501, 573–74 (no. 27). Roger Lancelyn Green notices the cartoon and ascribes it to Edward Bradley in *Lewis Carroll* (London: Bodley Head, 1960), p. 48; but according to Spielmann, p. 495, Bradley contributed nothing to *Punch* after 1856.

15. Caption: "THE DUKE OF CAMBRIDGE RECEIVING AN INVITATION TO A CHARITY DINNER ON HIS BIRTHDAY." On the table, a stack of papers marked "INVITATIONS"; beside it, a box marked "DINNER PILLS." Framed paintings of a pig and a hare are on the wall. February 24, 1844, was the seventieth birthday of Adolphus Frederick, duke of Cambridge, a son of George III and uncle of Queen Victoria. The duke was "most generous with his time . . . to an almost incredible number of charitable causes" (Roger Fulford, *Royal Dukes: The Father and Uncles of Queen Victoria* [London: Collins, 1973], p. 300). Apparently much of that time was spent banqueting, at the expense of the various foods shown here presenting an invitation inscribed "I.O.U."

16. *The Comic Almanack . . . First Series, 1835–1843* (London: Chatto, 1912), facing p. 289. For a dozen years, *Punch's Almanack* imitated and competed with Cruikshank's *Comic Almanack*, and in the end it was the survivor.

Caption: "December—'A Swallow at Christmas' (Rara avis in terris)." Since swallows are proverbially associated with summer, "a swallow at Christmas" must be a proverb or pseudoproverb for rarity—here given a punning interpretation.

Note the walking roast and pudding.

17. The cartoon is reprinted and the case identified in John Tenniel, *Cartoons from* Punch (London: Bradbury and Evans, n.d.), n.p.

18. Walter Shaw Sparrow published Müller's painting *Eel Bucks at Goring, 1843, with Boys Fishing* in *Angling in British Art through Five Centuries: Prints, Pictures, Books* (London: John Lane The Bodley Head, 1923), facing p. 116. For related works see p. 282; and also C. G. E. Bunt, *The Life and Work of William James Müller of Bristol* (Leigh-on-Sea, Eng.: F. Lewis, 1948).

Jeremy Maas gives the date 1838 for *Morning in the Meadows* in *Victorian Painters* (London: Barrie and Rockliff, 1969), p. 51. But Algernon Graves dated it 1851, and indicated that Thomas Sidney Cooper collaborated on the painting with Lee; see *The Royal Academy of Arts: A Complete Dictionary of Contributors*, 8 vols. (London: Henry Graves, 1905–6), 2:17; 5:149.

19. The quotation is from Keith A. P. Sandiford, *Great Britain and the Schleswig-Holstein Question, 1848–64: A Study in Diplomacy, Politics, and Public Opinion* (Toronto: University of Toronto Press, 1975), p. 118.

My account of the title page supposes that it was produced after the cabinet had announced its nonintervention policy in Parliament on 27 June. There is some evidence, perhaps unreliable, that it was designed before then.

20. The Russian bear has the spindly legs and military boots that Tenniel regularly gave to Czar Alexander II. The bandaged paw alludes to setbacks suffered in the Crimean War.

21. The Grand Duke Constantine, brother of Czar Alexander II, had paid a perfunctory courtesy visit to Queen Victoria, one "divested of any show or state," on 1 June 1857 (*Times*, 29 May 1857, p. 10; 1 June 1857, p. 9). The surname is taken from the hero of John Poole's farce, *Paul Pry* (1825), who was constantly making a nuisance of himself, and forever saying "I hope I don't intrude."

CHAPTER 2

1. *Alice's Adventures under Ground, Being a Facsimile of the Original Ms. Book Afterwards Developed into "Alice's Adventures in Wonderland"* (London: Macmillan & Co., 1886); the edition used in this chapter. Selwyn H. Goodacre and Denis Crutch describe various editions in "The 'Alice' Manuscript, and Its Facsimiles—An Annotated Hand List," *Jabberwocky* 7 (1978): 89–99; another facsimile edition has been published since, by Mayflower Books, New York (1980).

2. Williams and Madan, p. 110. This judgment has been perpetuated in the two later editions of the *Handbook*, passing muster with two more editors; and it has been invoked by Percy Muir, an authority on Victorian illustrated books. Probably this same comment of Madan's lies behind some skeptical remarks that Martin Gardner made in his introduction to a modern reprint of the Victorian facsimile edition: "No one knows whether Tenniel saw Carroll's drawings before he made his own sketches. There are obvious similarities here and there, but some such resemblances would have been hard to avoid." See *The Lewis Carroll Handbook*, ed. Roger Lancelyn Green (London: Oxford University Press), 1962, p. 134. Further revised by Crutch, p. 145. Percy Muir invokes Madan's comment in a letter to the editor of *Books*, Jan.–Feb. 1965, p. 31, objecting to an article by Frances Collingwood, "The Carroll-Tenniel Partnership," Nov.–Dec. 1964, pp. 232, 234–35. Martin Gardner, introduction to *Alice's Adventures under Ground* (New York: Dover, 1965), p. xi.

Despite this tradition of denial, a few critics do recognize the connection between Carroll's drawings and Tenniel's; for example, Frances Collingwood in the essay cited above; and Edward Hodnett in *Image and Text: Studies in the Illustration of English Literature* (London: Scolar Press, 1982), p. 175.

3. 20 December 1863; *Letters*, 1: 62.

4. *Diaries*, 1: 210, 212, 222.

5. October 12; *Diaries*, 1: 222. Hodnett, *Image and Text*, pp. 173-74, citing the opinion of Morton N. Cohen.

6. "Alice's Recollections of Carollian Days. As Told to Her Son, Caryl Hargreaves," *Cornhill*, n.s., 73 (1932):9.

7. Monkhouse, p. 28. On p. 10, Monkhouse credits Tenniel with much of his biographical information.

8. Collingwood, p. 96, mentions the borrowed "Natural History." Carroll's jerboa and two guinea pigs are conspicuous on p. 45 of *Alice's Adventures under Ground*.

Two of Tenniel's pencil drawings for figure 2.6 are in the Houghton Library at Harvard, and have been published in *Tenniel's Alice*, p. 35. In the earlier of these two drawings, the hedgehog is almost as round as that in Carroll's illustration, figure 2.5; in the later one it is sleeker, more like Bewick's rendition in figure 2.7.

9. Carroll was impressed with Tenniel's resourcefulness here; he drew attention to the device in commenting on the picture in *The Nursery "Alice"* (1890; rpt. New York: Dover, 1966), p. 27.

10. William Empson, *Some Versions of Pastoral* (London: Chatto & Windus, 1935) p. 271; Donald Rackin, "Laughing and Grief: What's so Funny About *Alice in Wonderland?*," *Lewis Carroll Observed*, ed. Edward Guiliano (New York: Clarkson N. Potter, 1976), p. 12.

11. Selwyn H. Goodacre, "Lewis Carroll's 1887 Corrections to *Alice*," *The Library* 28 (1973): 138.

CHAPTER 3

1. Carroll explains the King's expression even more clearly in *The Nursery "Alice"* (1890; rpt. New York: Dover, 1966), a simplified version for very young children. After suggesting that the reader "look at the big picture, at the beginning of this book," he comments: "The King is very grand, *isn't* he? But he doesn't look very *happy*. I think that big crown, on the top of his wig, must be *very* heavy and uncomfortable" (p. 50).

2. Tenniel colored the illustrations for *The Nursery "Alice"* himself, as Selwyn H. Goodacre demonstrates, citing an unpublished Carroll letter; "*The Nursery 'Alice'*: A Bibliographical Essay," *Jabberwocky* 4 (1975): 101. In the illustration of the royal procession in the garden (see chapter 6 below, figure 6.1), which takes place before the trial, the Knave has the same red nose—conspicuously red in *The Nursery "Alice."* It can also be seen later in the trial (fig. 3.4). The pepper-tart explanation was suggested to me by Kris Timian.

3. Charles H. Bennett, *The Fables of Aesop and Others, Translated into Human Nature* (1857; rpt. London: Chatto & Windus, 1875). Falconer Madan mentioned the "very remarkable and suggestive resemblance" in Williams and Madan, p. 18. Jeffrey Stern compared the various expressions and postures in a letter to the editor of *Jabberwocky* 7 (1978): 49.

4. Martin F. Tupper, *Proverbial Philosophy: Illustrated* (1854; rpt. London: Hatchard, n.d.), p. 65. In *Martin Tupper: His Rise and Fall* (London: Constable, 1949), p. 160, Derek Hudson remarked that this engraving "is parodied in the comic trial of the Knave of Hearts." Hudson also printed an uncommon letter from Tenniel (then aged 32) to Tupper, accepting the commission to do illustrations for the book:

Long ago, when I read the "Proverbial Philosophy" I felt it to be the subject of all others that I should like to illustrate, and I assure you that the feeling is greatly increased on a second reading. . . . As far as I have at present gone in the book *almost every subject suggests a picture*, so that I foresee considerable difficulty as regards selection— should the affair be definitely arranged, perhaps you will kindly assist me, by naming those that you would most wish to be illustrated. [P. 159]

This last comment bears on topics discussed in chapter 11 below.
Tenniel was one of several illustrators for the book.

5. A condemned man in chains, a draped corpse, and an executioner also dominate the left foreground of the cartoon, *The Spirit of Justice*, that won Tenniel a premium in the House of Lords competition (1845). See Monkhouse, facing p. 12.

CHAPTER 4

1. *Catalogue of Pictures of Old Masters, the Property of Miss Seymour . . . Which Will be Sold by Auction by Messrs. Christie, Manson & Woods . . . January 23, 1920*, lot 92. William A. Baillie-Grohman, "The Ugliest Woman in History," *Illustrated London News*, 25 December 1920, pp. 1080–81.

2. *The Land in the Mountains: Being an Account of the Past & Present of Tyrol, Its People and Its Castles* (Philadelphia: Lippincott, 1907), p. 78. Baillie-Grohman's main expertise was in the iconography of field sports.

3. W. A. Baillie-Grohman, "A Portrait of the Ugliest Princess in History," *Burlington Magazine* 38 (1921): 172–78.

4. Langford Reed, *The Life of Lewis Carroll* (London: W. & G. Foyle, 1932), p. 45. Lion Feuchtwanger, *The Ugly Duchess*, trans. Willa and Edwin Muir (New York: Viking, 1928). Falconer Madan mentioned the drawing, the painting, and the Feuchtwanger novel on p. 16 of the pamphlet *Supplement* (London: Oxford University Press, 1935) that he issued to Williams and Madan. There Carroll's "Duchess" became "the Ugly Duchess." See also William Empson, *Some Versions of Pastoral* (London: Chatto & Windus, 1935), pp. 273, 275, 276, and esp. 288.

5. Lennon, p. 112.

6. *Annotated Alice*, p. 82.

7. Martin Davies, *Early Netherlandish School*, 2d ed., National Gallery Catalogues (London: National Gallery, 1955), pp. 70–73, no. 5769. This article is not much enlarged in the third edition (1968), pp. 92–95, to which the following account refers.
Davies prefers the spelling "Quinten Massys"; it will be used here except in quotation from other sources.
Davies's suggestion that the painting is a copy has been endorsed by Hugh T. Broadley, "The Mature Style of Quinten Massys" (Ph.D. diss., New York University 1961), pp. 138–40; and by Andrée de Bosque, *Quentin Metsys* (Brussels: Arcade, 1975), p. 230.

8. Kenneth Clark, *A Catalogue of the Drawings of Leonardo da Vinci in the Collection of His Majesty the King at Windsor Castle*, 2 vols. (New York: Macmillan, 1935), 1:70–71, no. 12492. *The Drawings of Leonardo da Vinci in the Collection of Her Majesty the Queen at Windsor Castle*, 3 vols.(London: Phaidon, 1968), 1:83.

9. Gustav Friedrich Waagen, *Treasures of Art in Great Britain: Being an Account of the Chief Collections of Paintings, Drawings, Sculptures, Illuminated Mss., &c. &c.*, 4 vols. (1854; rpt. London: Cornmarket, 1970), 2:243. Waagen had seen the painting in the collection of Henry Danby Seymour during his visit to England in 1850. He reported it as follows:

QUENTIN MATSYS.—A frightful old woman; half-length figure, larger than life, painted with fearful truth in his later brown flesh-tones. Greatly resembling a caricature of a similar kind drawn by Leonardo da Vinci.

For Carroll's remark see *The Russian Journal and Other Selections from the Works of Lewis Carroll*, ed. John Francis McDermott (1935; rpt. New York: Dover, 1977), p. 78.

10. Erwin Panofsky, *Early Netherlandish Painting: Its Origins and Character,* The Charles Eliot Norton Lectures, 1947–1948, 2 vols. (Cambridge: Harvard University Press, 1953), 1:356. Ernst Gombrich, "Leonardo's Grotesque Heads," *Leonardo: Saggi e Richerche* (Rome: Instituto Puligrafico dello Stato, 1954), pp. 199–219.

11. A. H. Scott-Elliot, "Caricature Heads after Leonardo da Vinci in the Spencer Collection," *Bulletin of the New York Public Library* 62 (1958):283.

12. Besides the copy now in the National Gallery, there have been several other painted copies of the Massys original. According to Davies there are, or were in the nineteenth century, two copies in France (one copied from the other); and de Bosque mentions a Viennese copy. Given their locations, it is unlikely that Tenniel saw any of them.

13. "Champfleury" (Jules Fleury Husson), "Anatomie du Laid d'après Léonard de Vinci," *Gazette des Beaux-Arts*, ser. 2, 19 (1879): 198–99.

14. *Alumni Oxonienses* (Oxford: Parker and Co., 1888).

15. *The Ruskin Family Letters*, ed. Van Akin Burd, 2 vols. (Ithaca: Cornell University Press, 1973); see index.

16. According to Monkhouse, p. 10, Tenniel told him that he had been "very much interested in costume and armour, and studied them in the reading room and print room of the British Museum, where he laid the foundation of that knowledge of both, which has been of such great advantage to him as the cartoonist of *Punch*."

17. Figure 4.7: January–June 1852, p. 42. Figure 4.8: 26 July 1856, p. 39. Figure 4.9: 3 November 1860, p. 178. The prototype for figure 4.9 is the monumental effigy of Beatrice, Countess of Arundel (d. 1439), in the church at Arundel. Drawings of the head and headdress appear in the anonymous *History of British Costume* (London: Charles Knight, 1834), p. 189, and F. W. Fairholt's *Costume in England* (London: Chapman and Hall, 1846), p. 182. Both derive from pl. 105 in C. A. Stothard's *The Monumental Effigies of Great Britain* (London: privately printed, 1817), which may be Tenniel's immediate source. Both the anonymous historian and Fairholt emphasize how "ugly" the style was. A photograph of the effigy appears in Arthur Gardner's *Alabaster Tombs of the Pre-Reformation Period in England* (Cambridge: University Press, 1940), fig. 188. "The countess wears the most marvellous spreading head-dress . . . some 22 in. across" (p. 59).

18. Thomas Wright, *A History of Caricature & Grotesque in Literature and Art* (London: Virtue, 1865), p. 102. (Published in January 1865, according to the *Publishers' Circular*; a few copies have "1864" on the title page.) *Art-Journal*, n.s., 2 (1863): 143. A photograph of the misericord appears in Francis Bond, *Wood Carvings in English Churchs: Misericords* (London: Oxford University Press, 1910), p. 180.

CHAPTER 5

1. Lewis Carroll, *The Nursery "Alice"* (1890; rpt. New York: Dover, 1966), pp. 37–38. The past-tense verbs suggest that Carroll thinks of the sign as operating *within* the world of the fiction, as well as—or before—operating on the reader. That is, the other characters in the story could know, by interpreting the straw on his head, that the March Hare was mad.

The colored illustration of the tea-party in *The Nursery "Alice"* was adapted from the original black-and-white wood engraving that the Dalziel Brothers prepared after Tenniel's design. Tenniel's other drawing of the March Hare, near the end of the tea-party chapter in *Alice's Adventures*, shows the same view of his head with every straw in place.

2. John Boydell, *Collection of Prints, from Pictures Painted for the Purpose of Illustrating the Dramatic Works of Shakespeare*, 2 vols. (London, 1803), 2: pl. 45 (detail).

3. *Punch* 20 (Jan.–June 1851): 223.

4. *Pictorial Edition of the Works of Shakspere*, ed. Charles Knight, 7 vols. (London, n.d.), 1: 464. Boydell, *Collection of Prints*, 2:pl. 40 (detail).

5. Garrick wore a "crown of straw" over his theatrical wig; see Frederick Hawkins, "*Lear* on the Stage," *English Illustrated Magazine* 10 (1892–93): 161. Possibly the straw had been woven into the shape of an arched crown, as in the Hogarth illustration cited below. For the "straw scepter," see Marvin Rosenberg, *The Masks of King Lear* (Berkeley: University of California Press, 1972), p. 267. For Tenniel's interest in the theater see Jacquelin Knight, "The Theatre of John Tenniel," *Theatre Arts Monthly* 12 (1928): 111–18.

6. Forrest Reid credits the "Illustrations to Shakespeare" to Tenniel in *Illustrators of the Eighteen Sixties* (1928; rpt. New York: Dover, 1975), p. 27.

7. "At a wake, fair, or market you encountered quite a different Tom o' Bedlam [from the professional beggar]—also an imitation of an original. Here he was the merriest of madcaps, whooping, leaping, gambolling, decorated with ribbons and patches, 'crowned with weeds and flowers' " (Edward Geoffrey O'Donoghue, *The Story of Bethlehem Hospital from Its Foundation in 1247* [London: T. Fisher Unwin, 1914], p. 135). This account may connect with the "wild man," discussed below.

8. John Bright as a mad jackass crowned with straw: *Punch* 24 (Jan.–June 1853): 85. A cabdriver in a madhouse: 25 (July–Dec. 1853):53. Big Ben "cracked": 37 (15 Oct. 1859): 154. Fig. 5.9: 26 (Jan.–June 1854): 93. Nicholas I as a mad dog: 26 (Jan.–June 1854): 100. For theatrical associations and two more illustrations, see *Punch* 4 (January–June 1843):254; and 8 (January–June 1845):172.

9. O'Donoghue, *Bethlehem Hospital*, pp. 18 (Fox), 284 (Burke). Rowlandson's caricature of Fox (fig. 5.10 here) is erroneously attributed by O'Donaghue to Gillray; see M. Dorothy George, *Catalogue of Political and Personal Satires*, vol. 6 (London: British Museum, 1938), p. 81, no. 6495; the caricature of Burke is described on p. 52, no. 8367A. See also Joseph Grego, *Rowlandson the Caricaturist*, 2 vols. (London: Chatto and Windus, 1880), 1:124.

10. *Hogarth's Graphic Works*, ed. Ronald Paulson, rev. ed., 2 vols. (New Haven: Yale University Press, 1970), 1:170 (commentary); 2, pl. 248.

11. W. Harrison Ainsworth, *Jack Sheppard* (1839; rpt. London: Routledge, 1854), facing p. 214. The text reads: "Cowering in a corner upon a heap of straw, sat his unfortunate mother. . . . Her head had been shaved, and around it was swathed a piece of rag, in which a few straws were stuck" (p. 214). A letter from Cruikshank to Ainsworth indicates that this passage—like much of Ainsworth's fiction—was composed under Cruikshank's direction: "For fear you might not recollect the attire of Jack's Mother I will just state that her head which is *shaved* is bound with a *rag* in which some straws are stuck for ornament" (quoted in J. R. Harvey, *Victorian Novelists and Their Illustrators* [New York: New York University Press, 1971], p. 37).

12. Figure 5.13, a heraldic engraving by Martin Schongauer, decorates the title page of *Wild Men in the Middle Ages: A Study in Art, Sentiment, and Demonology* by Richard Bernheimer (Cambridge: Harvard University Press, 1952), where it also appears as figure 47. Related engravings by Schongauer appear in Timothy Husband's *The Wild Man: Medieval Myth and Symbolism* (New York: Metropolitan Museum of Art, 1980), pp. 186–87. Apparently wild men did reappear "in masques and civic processions" at the start of the sixteenth century in England (Bernheimer, *Wild Men*, p. 71).

CHAPTER 6

1. Such crisp juxtaposition of text and illustration is common throughout the early editions, but often neglected in later editions. See chapter 12 below.

2. *Aspects of the Novel* (1927; rpt. New York: Harcourt, 1962), pp. 103–18.

3. Roderick F. McGillis speculates on this question in "Tenniel's Turned Rabbit: A Reading of *Alice* with Tenniel's Help," *English Studies in Canada* 3 (1977): 326–35. Possible answers that he considers include deliberate mystification on Tenniel's part, and symbolic function for the Rabbit as a social and sexual being.

4. From a pack of cards printed by Thomas de la Rue in 1832, which conformed to traditional designs. Once in the Thomas de la Rue and Co. Collection deposited in the British Museum; now in the playing-card museum maintained in Vitoria, Spain, by the publisher Heraclio Fournier. See *Playing Cards* by Roger Tilley (London: Weidenfeld and Nicolson, 1967), pp. 2, 68–69; *Museo de Naipes* (Vitoria, Spain: Heraclio Fournier, n.d.), p. 109, no. 176. Figures 6.16, 6.17, and 6.22 are from the same set.

5. Derek Hudson, *Lewis Carroll* (London: Constable, 1954), p. 157. Carroll did once strike up a conversation with the Prince Consort, and was proud of it. And on 1 July 1865, while *Alice's Adventures* was being readied for the press, Carroll made the following entry in his diary: "Left for Windsor. . . . Walked in the Park in the afternoon; met the Queen driving in an open carriage, and got a bow from her all to myself."

6. Figure 6.11: January–June 1851, title page. Figure 6.12 (July–December 1851, p. 38): pointing with pride at the spectacle are Mr. Punch and Prince Albert. Albert had proposed the International Exhibition that the Crystal Palace was built to house, and he saw the idea through to completion.

7. Figure 6.13 is reprinted by courtesy of Brighton Reference Library, East Sussex. Evidently it is a detail from a print published in 1833; see Antony Dale, *Fashionable Brighton, 1820–1860* (Newcastle upon Tyne: Oriel Press, 1967), pl. 74; see also pp. 153–55. Figure 6.14 is taken from the *Gardener's Magazine* 7 (1831): 693; see John Hix, *The Glass House* (Cambridge, Mass.: MIT Press, 1974), p. 112. See also Stefan Koppelkamm, *Glasshouses and Wintergardens of the Nineteenth Century*, trans. Kathrine Talbot (New York: Rizzoli, 1981), p. 19, for contemporary comments on the style.

8. Figures 6.18 and 6.19 are from *The King and Queen of Hearts*, a booklet for children published anonymously in London in 1806, and reprinted in *The Works of Charles and Mary Lamb*, ed. E. V. Lucas, 7 vols. (New York: Putnam, 1903), 3:336–50. Probably the engravings (a series of sixteen) were by William Mulready, and preexisted a verse elaboration of the nursery rhyme that Charles Lamb attached to them. Each phrase of the original rhyme served as an illustration title. Figure 6.18 appears under the title "The King of Hearts."

Mulready's Queen wears the costume typical of the queen of hearts.

Notice, too, in the first illustration, that the composition of the two figures anticipates their composition in figure 6.1, including the Queen's outstretched left hand. It is possible that Tenniel knew this booklet. Figure 6.19, titled "And vow'd he'd steal no more," has affinities with figure 3.1, especially as regards the Knave's profile.

If Carroll knew of this booklet, he could have derived the Queen's tyrannical and murderous personality from that of the King, as implied in the verses Lamb wrote for figure 6.18:

> Behold the King of Hearts how gruff
> The monarch stands, how square, how bluff!
> When our eighth Harry ruld this land,
> Just like this King did Harry stand;
> And just so amourous, sweet, and willing,
> As this Queen stands, stood Anna Bullen.

This ominous note turns out to be of no consequence in the story, even as the Queen's commands are of no consequence in *Alice's Adventures*. Rather, Lamb is remarking on the resemblance between the standard playing-card king of hearts and the famous Holbein portrait of Henry VIII.

Figure 6.20 appeared in *Songs for the Nursery* (London: Darton, 1851); it is reprinted in *The Oxford Nursery Rhyme Book*, ed. Iona and Peter Opie (1955; rpt. Oxford: Clarendon Press, 1977). Note the heart-shaped fan in the Queen's right hand, perhaps noticed by Tenniel before he designed figure 6.1.

Figure 6.21, which shows the Knave of Hearts administering smelling salts to the Queen on her having discovered the theft of the tarts, is from *The Queen of Hearts Alphabet* (London: Read, Brooks and Co., [c. 1865]). The drawings, roughly contemporary with Tenniel's, were by Percy Cruikshank, George Cruikshank's nephew. Reprinted by Iona and Peter Opie in *Three Centuries of Nursery Rhymes and Poetry for Children*, an exhibition catalogue (London: National Book League, 1973), illustrating item 462.

Figures 6.20 and 6.21 are reprinted here by courtesy of Iona Opie.

9. For a more conservative account of the difference, published the same year as *Alice's Adventures*, see E. S. Taylor, *The History of Playing Cards, With Anecdotes of Their Use in Conjuring, Fortune-Telling, and Card-Sharping* (London, 1865; rpt. Rutland, Vt.: Tuttle, 1973), p. 473. In fortune-telling the queen of hearts "is a model of sincere affection, devotion, and prudence"; the queen of spades "is a person not to be provoked with impunity, never forgetting an injury, and having a considerable spice of malice in her composition." Strictly speaking, "sickness and death" are attributes not of the queen but of the ace of spades (p. 472). But widows (Queen Victoria, Gertrude) are always represented by the queen of spades (p. 471).

Carroll's own drawing of the Queen (fig. 6.4) bears reexamination in this context. The bodice design matches that of the queen of hearts, though without the checkered patterning. The triangular panel at the back of the gown may derive from the queen of spades. It is hard to say what Carroll was doing; but Tenniel took a full ensemble of details from the queen of spades.

CHAPTER 7

1. Tenniel began to work on *Looking-Glass* in 1869 or January 1870, and finished the latter half of 1871. See *Diaries*, 2: 280, 286, 303.

2. Spielmann, p. 329. Spielmann had interviewed Tenniel in 1889 about his general procedures working for *Punch* (pp. 461–66); they may have dealt with the supposed caricature then. But the phrase, "says Sir John Tenniel," suggests that Spielmann is quoting from writing. In his preface, written late in 1895, Spielmann reports that he had spent "four years . . . engaged upon this book," corresponding with "hundreds" of informants; so if Tenniel responded in writing he probably did so in the early nineties. Either way, he would have made this disclaimer to Spielmann some two decades after he drew the illustrations in question.

3. Spielmann, pp. 328–29; also Leonée Ormond, *George Du Maurier* (Pittsburgh: University of Pittsburgh Press, 1969), pp. 164, 168–69.

4. Harry Furniss, *The Confessions of a Caricaturist*, 2 vols. (New York: Harper, 1902), 1:300. (Furniss thought that others had been too quick to find personal caricatures in his own cartoons, and so he appreciated Tenniel's disclaimer.) Sarzano, p. 21. R. G. G. Price, *A History of* Punch (London: Collins, 1957), p. 74. Arthur Prager, *The Mahogany Tree: An Informal History of "Punch"* (New York: Hawthorn, 1979), p. 81.

5. An illustrated volume rubric from *Punch*, reproduced and analyzed by Prager, *Mahogany Tree*, p. 30.

6. See n. 1.

7. Spielmann, pp. 463, 466. Tenniel did concede that he would study photographs, to capture an unfamilar face or uniform "and so on."

8. Collingwood, p. 130. Presumably Carroll used the word "whiskers" in the old sense, denoting *moustache*, not in the new Victorian sense, denoting hair grown on the cheeks and sides of the face. Otherwise Tenniel did comply with this suggestion—though not with the suggestion about the Knight's age.

9. John Pudney, *Lewis Carroll and His World* (New York: Scribners, 1976), p. 77. In *Lewis Carroll: A Biography* (New York: Schocken, 1979), Anne Clark also characterizes Tenniel's White Knight as "a self-portrait of the artist" (p. 173).

10. A full-page portrait in Spielmann, p. 462.

CHAPTER 8

1. Crutch, p. 61. This is the best known instance of Carroll's custom of showing the Tenniel illustrations to friends before publication. For other instances see *The Lewis Carroll Picture Book*, ed. Stuart Dodgson Collingwood (1899; rpt. Detroit: Tower, 1971), p. 360; and *Diaries*, 2:288.

2. Alexander L. Taylor, *The White Knight: A Study of C. L. Dodgson (Lewis Carroll)* (Edinburgh: Oliver & Boyd, 1952), p. 80.

3. Rousseau objected to the French custom of rearing children on La Fontaine's *Fables*, for the details of the stories were beyond the understanding of children; also, children would perversely mistake or misapply the moral. In general he disliked burdening children with books, preferring to teach directly from experience. In their book *Practical Education* (1798), where they adapted many of Rousseau's theories to the English scene, Maria and Richard Edgeworth condemned fabulous stories and anticipated Figuier's recommendation that children study natural history instead. Wordsworth, in a well-known passage in *The Prelude* (5:332–33; drafted 1805–6), derided modern educational programs like the Edgeworths', because a diet of science to the exclusion of fables and fairy tales was sure to stunt a child's imaginative and emotional development.

4. Louis Figuier, *The World before the Deluge* (London: Chapman and Hall, 1865). A second edition, omitting Figuier's polemical preface, was published in London

and New York by Cassell, Petter and Galpin (1866). The edition published by Appleton and Co. in New York in 1866, printed by William Clowes and Sons in London, appears to be identical (save for the title page) to the Chapman and Hall first edition of 1865.

Riou's fantastic illustrations proved to be very popular. Redrawn, and without attribution, they appeared in Alexander Winchell's *Sketches of Creation* (New York: Harper, 1870; often reprinted), from which they were borrowed by Sophie B. Herrick for her book of paleontology for young people, *The Earth in Ages Past* (New York: American Book, 1888), which was serialized in *St. Nicholas*, the popular children's magazine. Professional naturalists, like Henry Woodward, would later discredit these "highly sensational views of extinct monsters," but this vein of fantasy has become a staple of children's literature.

It happens that H. C. Hutchinson, in whose book Woodward's comment appeared, opened his popular account of paleontology by citing the Jabberwock: "We shall, perhaps, find this antique world quite as strange as the fairy-land of Grimm or Lewis Carroll. True, it was not inhabited by 'slithy toves' or 'jabberwocks,' but by real beasts, of whose shapes, sizes, and habits much is already known. . . . And yet, real as it all is, this antique world—this panorama of scenes that have for ever passed away—is a veritable fairy-land." These comments are much in the spirit of Figuier's preface. H. N. Hutchinson, *Extinct Monsters: A Popular Account of Some of the Larger Forms of Ancient Animal Life*, rev. ed. (London: Chapman and Hall, 1893), p. 1; Woodward's dismissal of Riou is on p. v.

5. Figure 8.8: 20 (Jan.–June 1851):91. Figure 8.9: 23 (July–Dec. 1852): 85. Figure 8.10: 25 (July–Dec. 1853): 161. Figure 8.11: 21 (July–Dec. 1851): 67. Figure 8.12: 21 (July–Dec. 1851): 133. Figure 8.13: 22 (Jan.–June 1852): 105.

6. Francis Huxley, *The Raven and the Writing Desk* (New York: Harper & Row, 1976), p. 68.

7. "The Saints of Old. (That is, of the Dark Ages.) A Chant for the Times," *Punch* 20 (January–June 1851): 122. This satiric verse is an instance of the anti-Catholic feeling provoked by the so-called "Papal Aggression" of 1850, in which Nicholas Wiseman was made cardinal archbishop of Westminster.

8. Thomas Wright, *A History of Caricature & Grotesque in Literature and Art* (London: Virtue, 1865), p. 299; previously published in the *Art-Journal*, n.s., 3 (1864): 117. This is the same work that included Fairholt's engraving of the grotesque misericord, discussed in chapter 4 as a possible source for Tenniel's Duchess.

In drawing St. Anthony, Fairholt may have copied Williams. For a discussion of the "outline style" of drawing, see chapter 4 of William Vaughan's *German Romanticism and English Art* (New Haven: Yale University Press, 1979).

9. *Modern Painters*, in *The Works of John Ruskin*, ed. E. T. Cook and Alexander Wedderburn, 39 vols. (London: George Allen, 1903–12), 4:373 (from a manuscript), 86; 7:309.

10. Carl Linfert, *Hieronymus Bosch*, trans. Robert Erich Wolf (New York: Abrams, 1971), p. 74.

During his visit to the Royal Museum in Berlin in 1867 Carroll noticed "several [paintings] well known from engravings, such as St. Anthony's temptation"; *The Russian Journal and Other Selections from the Works of Lewis Carroll*, ed. John Francis McDermott (1935; rpt. New York: Dover, 1977), p. 78. I have not been able to identify the painting.

CHAPTER 9

1. William Empson, *Some Versions of Pastoral* (London: Chatto & Windus, 1935), p. 256.

2. Sarzano, p. 21; *Annotated Alice*, p. 218; *Alice in Wonderland*, ed. Donald J. Gray (New York: Norton, 1971), p. 130.

3. Lennon, p. 184; *Annotated Alice*, p. 288. Michael Patrick Hearn, in his essay "*Alice's* Other Parent: John Tenniel as Lewis Carroll's Illustrator," *American Book Collector* 4 (May–June, 1983): 18, attributes the Disraeli and Gladstone interpretations to "some early reviewers"—not identified.

4. *Diaries*, 1: 237; 2: 277; Alison Lurie, "On the Subversive Side," *Times Literary Supplement*, 28 March 1980, p. 353.

5. Figure 9.2: 20 May 1871. Figure 9.3: 27 May 1871. Figure 9.4: 1 July 1871. Figure 9.5: 5 August 1871. Tenniel began sketching for *Looking-Glass* in January 1870, but apparently had not finished work by August 1871.

6. Reproduced from Phillip James, *Children's Books of Yesterday* (London: The Studio, 1933), p. 113. A similar reverse drawing of this scene is reproduced in *Tenniel's Alice*, p. 53. Tenniel included a very rough sketch of this scene in a letter to Carroll, reproduced in Collingwood, p. 147; see figure 10.5.

7. Odell Shepard, *The Lore of The Unicorn* (New York: Barnes and Noble, 1967), p. 70. Figure 9.7 is from Burke's *Peerage and Baronetage*, 31st ed. (London: Harrison, 1869), p. xv.

8. October 7, 1871. The cartoon and a poem on the facing page make swimming instruction a matter of patriotic duty. The quotation in the caption plays on the words of James Thomson's *The Seasons*, "Spring," 1153.

9. Figure 9.9: 15 June 1861. Figure 9.10: 23 October 1858.

10. Raymond Lister, *Victorian Narrative Paintings* (London: Museum Press, 1966), pp. 52-53. For Egg's friendship with Leech and Lemon (!) see *A Victorian Canvas: The Memoirs of W. P. Frith, R. A.*, ed. Nevile Wallis (London: Geoffrey Bles, 1957), pp. 60–61. According to the City of Birmingham City Museums and Art Gallery, who now own the painting, it entered a private collection in May of 1863, the year after it was painted.

11. Millais painted a sequel, *My Second Sermon* (1864), which was also engraved and published in 1865: it showed the same sitter (Millais' daughter, Effie), in the same setting and costume, with her hat at her side, drowsing off. See *Millais: An Exhibition* (Liverpool: Walker Art Gallery, 1967), pp. 46–47; and Hilary Guise, *Great Victorian Engravings: A Collector's Guide* (London: Astragal Books, 1980), p. 134. Both paintings are reproduced by Geoffrey Millais, *Sir John Everett Millais* (London: Academy Editions, 1979), pp. 72–73.

12. Figure 9.14 is from *Punch's Almanack* for 1868. The fashion for porkpie hats lasted approximately from 1855 to 1865 (*OED*); the hat was fashionable for children before it was for adults (Anne Buck, *Victorian Costume and Costume Accessories* [New York: Nelson, 1961], p. 117). The photograph shows the daughters of the fourth marquess of Bath; published by Adeline Hartcup, *Children of the Great Country Houses* (London: Sidgwick & Jackson, 1982), p. 131.

In his children's book *Little Annie and Jack in London* (1869), Walter Crane included a drawing of a brother and sister and their parents seated in a railway compartment. The point of view is the same as in figure 9.1. The girl, about Alice's age, sits in the same corner, though turned to her left; she wears a similar hairdo, and hat (though without the feather), and bow tie, and muff. Reproduced in Rodney K. Engen, *Walter Crane as a Book Illustrator* (London: Academy Editions, 1975), p. 30; cf. also p. 29.

13. Figures 9.17 and 9.18 are from vol. 20 (January–June 1851): 20, 61. For an account of the decorated page in Germany and England see William Vaughan, *German Romanticism and English Art* (New Haven: Yale University Press, 1979), pp. 155–76.

14. In the Rossetti painting, of course, the grape vines are emblematic, prefiguring the Passion. And in figure 9.21 they connote husbandry and harvest, aspects of the work of education. But these are exceptional uses of the ornamental motif.

Conventional flourishes of ivy also ornament the cover to the illustrated manuscript of *Alice's Adventures under Ground*, which Carroll specially prepared for Alice Liddell in 1863 and 1864, and which Tenniel evidently knew.

CHAPTER 10

1. On 2 May 1864, before Tenniel had begun work on the pictures, Carroll sent him "the first piece of slip set up for *Alice's Adventures*—from the beginning of Chap: III." Four days later he sent to the printer "a batch of MS. from the first chapter of *Alice's Adventures.*" Much later Carroll records sending Tenniel galleys of *Through the Looking-Glass* (15 January 1871).

2. W. H. Bond, "The Publication of *Alice's Adventures in Wonderland,*" *Harvard Library Bulletin* 10 (1956): 306–24.

Selwyn H. Goodacre emphasizes a different printing defect—inferior ink penetrating the page and marring the pictures—in "The 1865 *Alice*: A New Appraisal and a Revised Census," *Soaring with the Dodo: Essays on Lewis Carroll's Life and Art,* ed. Edward Guiliano and James R. Kincaid (Silver Spring, Md: Lewis Carroll Society of North America, 1982), pp. 79–81. Tenniel objected to "the disgraceful printing"; Carroll may have been wrong in interpreting the objection as one against "the printing of the pictures." See also Edward Hodnett, *Image and Text: Studies in the Illustration of English Literature* (London: Scolar Press, 1982), p. 172.

Carroll long continued to respect Tenniel's opinion in such technical matters: in 1871, responding to a complaint of Tenniel's, he urged Macmillan to take extra care in the printing of *Through the Looking-Glass* (Crutch, p. 67); and in 1896, while the People's Edition of the two books was being prepared, Carroll arranged for Tenniel to "examine proofs of the pictures," which were printed from new electrotypes made from the original wood engravings (*Diaries,* 2: 528). Three years before that, Carroll had independently complained to Macmillan about the careless printing of the illustrations in a new issue of *Through the Looking-Glass* (Selwyn H. Goodacre, "Lewis Carroll's Rejection of the 60th Thousand of *Through the Looking-Glass,*" *Book Collector* 24 [1975]: 251–59).

3. *Diaries,* 1: 234. Carroll at first thought that doing it all again meant reengraving all the pictures, which would have required Tenniel to draw them all again on woodblocks, but such heroic measures were not needed. The blocks used in the first printing were adequate in themselves; all they needed was more careful treatment. However, the type was entirely reset, to correct a variety of defects. Tenniel gave the new printing his approval—but not before Macmillan had already begun publication (Bond, "The Publication of *Alice's Adventures,*" p. 312).

4. *Letters,* 1: 74.

5. See Carroll's own chronology, reproduced in the *Letters,* 1: 72; and also the *Diaries.*

6. *Times,* 7 March 1931, p. 9; 10 March 1931, p. 10; 13 March 1931, p. 10; 19 March 1931, p. 10; 20 March 1931, p. 10; see also 12 March 1931, p. 8.

7. Falconer Madan appropriately hedged his report about Carter: "The prototype of the Mad Hatter is believed to be a Mr. Theophilus Carter" (Williams and Madan, p. 21). Martin Gardner was less cautious, asserting that "There is good reason to believe that Tenniel adopted a suggestion of Carroll's that he draw the Hatter to resemble" Carter (*Annotated Alice,* p. 93). Matters become complicated when biographers take into account an enigmatic remark that S. D. Collingwood made in his early *Life and Letters of Lewis Carroll* (1898; rpt. 1899).

According to Collingwood, during Carroll's undergraduate days at Christ Church he was assigned to a dining table along with an unidentified person who was to become the prototype of the Mad Hatter. Derek Hudson assumed that any reference to a Mad Hatter prototype must be a reference to Theophilus Carter: therefore in the first edition of his biography of Carroll he identified Carter as having been "once of Christ Church"—only "later a furniture dealer in the High." Roger Lancelyn Green, failing to find Carter listed in *Alumni Oxonienses,* concluded that he "may simply have waited" on Carroll's table, and identified Carter unequivocally as "at one time a servitor at Christ Church and later a furniture dealer with a shop in the High at Oxford." For the second edition of his biography, Hudson revised his description accordingly: now Carter was "once a servitor of Christ Church" before he became a furniture dealer. But the tone of Collingwood's original remark naturally suggests that his reference was to an undergraduate colleague of Carroll's, not to a waiter: "In those days the undergraduates dining in hall were divided into 'messes.' Each mess consisted of about half a dozen men, who had a table to themselves.... In Mr. Dodgson's mess were Philip Pusey [son of Edward Pusey, the

theologian], the late Rev. G. C. Woodhouse, and, among others, one who still lives in 'Alice in Wonderland' as the 'Hatter.'" The idea that Carter was a servitor at Christ Church is a conjecture made to reconcile Collingwood's reference to the Mad Hatter with Greene's. But there is no evidence that either Collingwood or Greene was right about the Mad Hatter, let alone that they both were. (Collingwood, p. 47. Derek Hudson, *Lewis Carroll* [London: Constable, 1954], p. 144; 2d ed., p. 126. Roger Lancelyn Green, ed., *Alice's Adventures in Wonderland and Through the Looking-Glass* [1971; rpt. London: Oxford University Press, 1976], p. 258.)

Hudson, in the second edition of his biography, pp. 63–64, quotes extensively from an obituary article by the Reverend G. J. Cowley-Brown, one of Carroll's classmates, which was evidently Collingwood's source for the anecdote. The context of Cowley-Brown's reference to the Mad Hatter is a roll call of undergraduate colleagues.

In a letter to the editor of *Books,* January–February 1965, pp. 30–31, P. H. Muir mentions yet another candidate: "It has been suggested that Edward Bradley, author of the 'Verdant Green' books . . . bore a strong resemblance to the Mad Hatter." Tenniel would have known Bradley from his early years at *Punch,* to which Bradley had contributed occasional drawings; see Spielmann, pp. 491–95. The photograph of Bradley on p. 492 is inconclusive.

8. Williams and Madan, p. 22.

9. Lennon, pp. 112, 314. John Pudney, *Lewis Carroll and His World* (New York: Scribners, 1976), p. 77. Hudson, *Lewis Carroll,* 2d ed., p. 119. Anne Clark, *Lewis Carroll: A Biography* (New York: Schocken, 1979), p.135; also her biography of Alice Liddell, *The Real Alice: Lewis Carroll's Dream Child* (London: Michael Joseph, 1981), pp. 105, 106. Graham Ovenden, ed., *The Illustrators of Alice in Wonderland and Through the Looking Glass* (London: Academy Editions, 1972), p. 103. In his introduction to this book, John Davis says that Tenniel's illustrations were "undoubtedly" based on Miss Badcock, though he "probably worked straight from the photograph" (p. 8).

10. Arthur A. Adrian, *Mark Lemon: First Editor of "Punch"* (London: Oxford University Press, 1966), pp. 143–44. Adrian notices the inconsistency, but tries to explain it away by conjecturing that Tenniel "made the drawings of Kate Lemon in 1864, told her he was using them for Alice, and then put them aside for later use in *Through the Looking-Glass.*"

Kate Lemon's daughter, Mrs. Nora Lemon Trevor, further claimed that as a child she had read a copy of *Alice in Wonderland* (sic) that Tenniel had inscribed to Kate Lemon with his thanks for her "being his model"; see "Three Models in Wonderland," *Daily Telegraph and Morning Post,* 7 July 1965, p. 16, and "Alice: The Truth," *Sunday Times,* 11 July 1965, p. 7. Mrs. Trevor was then eighty-three.

11. Jeffrey Stern, "Lewis Carroll the Pre-Raphaelite: 'Fainting in Coils,'" *Lewis Carroll Observed,* ed. Edward Guiliano (New York: Clarkson N. Potter, 1976), pp. 161–80.

Alice Liddell was aware of a deliberate difference between Tenniel's Alice and herself, according to Caryl Hargreaves, "Alice's Recollections of Carrollian Days. As Told to Her Son, Caryl Hargreaves," *Cornhill,* n.s., 73 (1932):9: "One point, which was not settled for a long time and until after many trials and consultations [between Carroll and Tenniel], was whether Alice in Wonderland should have her hair cut straight across her forehead as Alice Liddell had always worn it, or not. Finally it was decided that Alice in Wonderland should have no facial resemblance to her prototype."

Figure 10.2 is the photograph of Alice Liddell by Lewis Carroll that Carroll affixed to the end of the gift manuscript of *Alice's Adventures.*

12. August 24, 1866; *Letters,* 1:94.

13. Williams and Madan, p. 238.

14. May 19, 1868; *Letters,* 1:120. In the same sentence, Carroll goes on to rule out the Pre-Raphaelite painter Arthur Hughes, because "he has not, so far as I know, any turn for grotesque." For Hughes's relationship to George MacDonald and Carroll, see Stern, "Lewis Carroll the Pre-Raphaelite," pp. 172–75.

15. Ten years later Carroll discovered the work of A. B. Frost in the same magazine, which is how Frost came to illustrate Carroll's verse collection *Rhyme? and Reason?* (1883); see *Letters,* 1:298.

16. It has sometimes been said that, besides Doyle and Paton (and Proctor), Carroll also approached W. S. Gilbert, later famous as the librettist for the Savoy

operas. Carroll did admire some of Gilbert's magazine illustrations, signed "Bab"; and after Tenniel provided the identification, Carroll made inquiries about Gilbert; but Carroll never actually approached him. See *Letters*, 1:120.

Tenniel also identified Georgina Bowers as the artist who had recently begun publishing "sporting pictures" in *Punch* (*Diaries*, 2:267); but there is no evidence that Carroll offered her the commission.

17. Collingwood, p. 130. Carroll loathed "the unapproachable ugliness of 'crino-line,'" as he later described it to Harry Furniss; "I *hate* crinoline fashion." Harry Furniss, *The Confessions of a Caricaturist*, 2 vols. (New York: Harper, 1902), p. 107.

18. Tenniel's *Looking-Glass* chessmen are modifications of the English "Staunton" pattern, designed by Nathaniel Cook in 1835; it became the international standard. A representative Victorian set and the illustrations from the pattern book published by the original manufacturer are reproduced by A. E. J. Mackett-Beeson in *Chessmen* (New York: Putnam, 1968), pp. 34–35. Tenniel's Knights follow the Staunton type closely, especially in the illustrations early in the book, and so stand only two generations removed from the classical horses' heads of the Elgin marbles. But the skirts of Tenniel's chessmen are more corrugated and more voluminous than the bases in that pattern—less tapered and more like skirts. Tenniel also deprived the Kings of their crowns (significantly?), substituting instead coronets like those worn by the Queens.

The proofs reproduced by figures 10.3 and 10.4 are in the British Museum, MS. C247, vol. 28, fols. 673, 671; Edward Guiliano kindly brought them to my attention. Folios 674 and 672 are proofs that highlight the corrections (or revisions) made on these same woodblocks. Michael Patrick Hearn is preparing to publish these and other Dalziel proofs for the *Alice* books, now in the British Museum.

Tenniel's tracing-paper sketch of figure 10.3 (made to transfer the outlines of a previous paper sketch to the woodblock) is reproduced by Sarzano, p. 68.

For detailed accounts of Alice's changing wardrobe in the Tenniel illustrations, see F. Gordon Roe, *The Victorian Child* (London: Phoenix House, 1959), pp. 81–84; and Elizabeth Ewing, *History of Children's Costume* (New York: Scribners, 1977), pp. 96–98.

19. Harry Furniss, "Recollections of 'Lewis Carroll,'" *Strand Magazine*, April 1908, p. 51. Morton N. Cohen, "Lewis Carroll and the House of Macmillan," *Browning Institute Studies* 7 (1979): 31–70, esp. 61–63. Crutch, pp. 130–31.

20. Furniss, "Recollections," p. 50. Furniss varied the story slightly in *The Confessions of a Caricaturist*, 1:103: "Tenniel and other artists declared I would not work with Carroll for seven weeks!"

21. Dorothy Furniss, "New Lewis Carroll Letters," *Pearson's Magazine*, December 1930, pp. 635–36.

22. Collingwood, pp. 146, 148–49. Lewis Carroll, *The Wasp in a Wig: A "Suppressed" Episode of* Through the Looking-Glass and What Alice Found There, ed. Martin Gardner (New York: Lewis Carroll Society of North America, 1977). The quality and authenticity of this text are debated in a special issue of *Jabberwocky*, 7:3 (Summer 1978).

Percy Muir, drawing on Carroll's unpublished letters to Macmillan, has mentioned another instance of Carroll taking Tenniel's advice in preparing *Looking-Glass*. Apparently Carroll had considered having an illustrated title page, but Tenniel rejected the idea. Percy Muir, *English Children's Books: 1600 to 1900* (London: B. T. Batsford, 1954), p. 141.

23. Collingwood, p. 146. Tenniel was exaggerating, but not much; he contributed one illustration to S. C. Hall's *The Trial of Sir Jasper* (1873) and two new illustrations to Walter Thornbury's *Historical and Legendary Ballads and Songs* (1876).
Carroll's *Diaries* (2:337–38) record that in 1875 Tenniel "consented" to draw a frontispiece for a "little book of original puzzles etc. which I think of calling *Alice's Puzzle-Book*," but nothing came of this project.

CHAPTER 11

1. See Gleeson White, *English Illustration: The Sixties* (1897; rpt. Bath: Kingsmead, 1970), p. 107; Forrest Reid, *Illustrators of the Eighteen Sixties* (1928; rpt. New York: Dover, 1975), pp. 28–29; Percy Muir, *Victorian Illustrated Books* (New York: Praeger, 1971), pp. 109–10; William Vaughan, *German Romanticism and English Art* (New Haven: Yale University Press, 1979), pp. 155–76; Eric de Maré, *The Victorian Woodblock Illustrators* (London: Gordon Fraser, 1980), p. 146.

2. John Ruskin, *Ariadne Florentina: Six Lectures on Wood and Metal Engraving* (delivered in 1872); *The Works of John Ruskin*, ed. E.T. Cook and Alexander Wedderburn, 39 vols. (London: George Allen, 1903–12), 22:359–60. (Ruskin preferred, as more authentic and less mechanical, the wood-engraving technique of Thomas Bewick, who designed most of his own work and modeled his pictures directly with the white lines cut by the chisel.) See also John Jackson and W. A. Chatto, *A Treatise on Wood Engraving*, 2d ed. (London: Henry G. Bohn, 1861), pp. 561–62, 599–601; their account of the labor involved is more conservative than Ruskin's, but not much different.

3. Spielmann, pp. 463–64. Monkhouse, p. 8. A similar procedure was followed by Dickens's illustrator, Hablot Brown ("Phiz"); Edgar Browne, *Phiz and Dickens* (London: Nisbet, 1913), p. 164, as cited by Michel Steig, *Dickens and Phiz* (Bloomington: Indiana University Press, 1978), p. 16. The tracing-paper technique was also used by engravers, who probably devised it; see Thomas Gilks, *The Art of Wood Engraving: A Practical Handbook*, 3d ed. (London: Winsor and Newton, 1871), pp. 23–24.
During the sixties it became possible to transfer drawings from paper to the woodblock photographically, before engraving. Tenniel characteristically resisted this new procedure; he continued to prepare his *Punch* drawings as described well into the nineties. It was also possible to transfer drawings photographically from one block to another; see note 14 below.

4. So Eleanor Garvey and W. H. Bond imply in their introduction to *Tenniel's Alice*, p. 9.

5. Percy Muir, discussing a single one of these finished drawings, suggested that Tenniel executed it after the fact, as a collector's item; he cited precedents involving some of Tenniel's *Punch* cartoons (*Victorian Illustrated Books*, p. 110). Justin G. Schiller is currently preparing a catalogue of all drawings and picture proofs associated with the *Alice* books, and he believes that the highly finished drawings published in *Tenniel's Alice* were all done after the fact, for collectors; see his review in *Jabberwocky* 9 (1980): 104–7.

6. See their memoir *The Brothers Dalziel: A Record* (1901), reprinted with a foreword by Graham Reynolds (London: B. T. Batsford, 1978). See also Simon Houfe's introduction to *The Dalziel Family: Engravers and Illustrators* (London: Sotheby, 1978). Percy Muir devotes chapter 6 of *Victorian Illustrated Books* to "The Dalziel Era."

7. The Moxon illustrated Tennyson has been reprinted by the Scolar Press (London, 1976; a facsimile of the edition of 1866). It is the subject of *Tennyson and His Pre-Raphaelite Illustrators*, by George Somes Layard (London: Elliot Stock, 1894); "The Pre-Raphaelite Tennyson," by Richard L. Stein, *Victorian Studies* 24 (1981): 278–301; and "The Pre-Raphaelites and the Moxon *Tennyson*," by Jack T. Harris, *Journal of Pre-Raphaelite Studies* 3 (1983): 26–37. See also Harold G. Merriam, *Edward Moxon: Publisher of Poets* (New York: Columbia University Press, 1939), pp. 181–85; and June Steffensen Hagen, *Tennyson and His Publishers* (London: Macmillan & Co., 1979), pp. 100–106.

8. Tenniel's Alice and Hunt's Lady are also related by collateral descent. According to family tradition, Hunt's model for his drawing of the Lady was his mistress, Annie Miller. Miller, as represented in a drawing by Dante Gabriel Rossetti that Carroll photographed, strongly influenced Carroll's Pre-Raphaelite-esque drawings of Alice—which in turn had their influence on Tenniel's drawings. Carroll's photograph of Rossetti's drawing of Miller is reproduced by Jeffrey Stern, "Lewis Carroll the Pre-Raphaelite: 'Fainting in Coils,'" *Lewis Carroll Observed*, ed. Edward Guiliano (New York: Clarkson N. Potter, 1976), p. 169—juxtaposed there to a remarkably similar drawing by Carroll for *Alice's Adventures under Ground*. Regarding Miller as the model for Hunt's Lady, see Diana Holman-Hunt, *My Grandfather, His Wives and Loves* (London: Hamilton, 1969), p. 205; cited by Allan R. Life, "'Poetic Naturalism': Forrest Reid and the Illustrators of the Sixties," *Victorian Periodicals Newsletter*

10 (1977): 65, 68 (n. 46).

9. W. Holman Hunt, *Pre-Raphaelitism and the Pre-Raphaelite Brotherhood* (New York: Macmillan, 1906), 1:124–25.

Hunt's apology for artistic license in illustration recalls Reynold's defence of idealization in history painting: "A Painter must compensate the natural deficiencies of his art. He has but one sentence to utter, but one moment to exhibit. He cannot, like the poet or historian, expatiate. . . . " (Sir Joshua Reynolds, *Discourses on Art*, ed. Robert R. Wark, rev. ed. [New Haven: Yale University Press, 1975], p. 60 [Discourse 4; 1771]).

When Hunt reconstructed his conversation with Tennyson, some fifty years after the fact, he had just completed a painting of the Lady of Shalott that derived freely from the engraving. It would have amazed Tennsyon in its elaboration of iconographic details unprecedented in either the poem or the engraving. See Samuel J. Wagstaff, Jr., "Some Notes on Holman Hunt and The Lady of Shalott," *Wadsworth Athenaeum Bulletin*, 5th ser., no. 11 (1962): 1–21; and Udo Kultermann, "William Holman Hunt's 'The Lady of Shalott': Material for an Interpretation," *Pantheon* 38 (1980): 386–92.

10. *Letters of Dante Gabriel Rossetti*, ed. Oswald Doughty and John Robert Wahl, 4 vols. (Oxford: Clarendon Press, 1965–67), 1:239.

11. Cook and Wedderburn, *Works of John Ruskin*, 36:264–65.

12. Graham Greene, introduction to Charles Dickens, *Oliver Twist* (London: Hamish Hamilton, 1950), p. vii; as cited by Jane R. Cohen, *Charles Dickens and His Original Illustrators* (Columbus: Ohio State University Press, 1980), p. 234.

13. *Dante Gabriel Rossetti: His Family-Letters*, ed. William Michael Rossetti, 2 vols. (Boston: Roberts Brothers, 1895), 1:189–90. W. M. Rossetti later offered a supposedly authoritative account of "what Rossetti meant," distinguished from the description of St. Cecilia given by the poem (Virginia Surtees, *The Paintings and Drawings of Dante Gabriel Rossetti [1828–1882]: A Catalogue Raisonné*, 2 vols. [Oxford: Clarendon Press, 1971], 1:48).

14. *Letters*, 1:39. Moxon illustrated "The Lady of Shalott" with two engravings, the one by Hunt already discussed, and another by Rossetti, which is evidently the one referred to here.

Presumably what Carroll saw in Rossetti's studio was not a photograph of any preliminary drawing of "St. Cecilia" but rather one made from Rossetti's drawing on the block: late in 1856 Rossetti sent a copy of such a photograph to William Allingham (Rossetti, *Letters*, 1:315). Two of Rossetti's preliminary paper drawings for this illustration survive (Surtees, *Rossetti*, 1:48).

Carroll's perception may have been colored by Ruskin's complaint, published in *The Elements of Drawing* (1857), about the poor quality of the engraving for the Moxon edition, especially the engraving of the St. Cecilia drawing. The drawings had been "terribly spoiled in the cutting, and generally the best part, the expression of feature, [was] *entirely* lost. . . . This is especially the case in the St. Cecily . . . which would have been the best in the book had it been well engraved" (*Works* 15:224).

N. John Hall has published, on facing pages of his book *Trollope and His Illustrators* (New York: St. Martin's Press, 1980), pls. 33, 34, a Dalziel engraving of an illustration by J. E. Millais for Trollope's novel *The Small House at Allington* (1864), and a photograph of the "original pencil drawing on the [the] wood block." The engraving is a very close copy of the drawing, if not a line-for-line replication. The same is true of the four engravings that Dalziel made from four Millais drawings on wood that still survive, and that are reproduced by Mary Lutyens in her introduction to a reprint of the Dalziel volume, *The Parables of Our Lord and Saviour Jesus Christ* (1864; rpt. New York: Dover, 1975), pp. 20, 41, 48, 73 (cf. pp. xi, xiii, xxix, xxxi).

These four original wood blocks for *The Parables* survive because Dalziel—possibly for the first time—succeeded in copying the drawings photographically onto secondary wood blocks, which were the ones that actually got engraved; Dalziel then sold the original blocks to collectors for an added profit. So far as I know, Dalziel did not take such pains with any *Alice* drawings, if Tenniel did draw any directly on the wood. For technical information and speculation see Paul Fildes, "Phototransfer of Drawings in Wood-block Engraving," *Journal of the Printing Historical Society*, no. 5 (1969): 87–98.

15. But see note 5 above; Schiller cites this same illustration, maintaining that Tenniel copied 11.5 from 11.3.

Regarding another Alice drawing, owned by the Library of Congress, Edward

Hodnett makes the opposite, and more usual, assumption; see *Image and Text: Studies in the Illustration of English Literature* (London: Scolar Press, 1982), p. 182.

16. Harold Hartley quotes from Carroll's letter in "Lewis Carroll and His Artists and Engravers," *The Lewis Carroll Centenary in London, 1932*, ed. Falconer Madan (London: J. & E. Bumpus, 1932), p. 115. For the Dalziels' recollection of their dealings with Carroll see *The Brothers Dalziel*, p. 126.

17. Rossetti, *Letters*, 1:243. For the quotation see p. 318, and also p. 310.

Millais cooperated with the Dalziels on the Tennyson project more closely than Rossetti did, and he was lavish in praising their work on later commissions. See Mary Lutyens, ed., "Letters from Sir John Everett Millais, Bart., P.R.A. (1829–1896) and William Holman Hunt, O. M. (1827–1910) in the Henry E. Huntington Library, San Marino, California," *The Forty-Fourth Volume of the Walpole Society, 1972–1974* (1974), pp. 1–93, esp. pp. 17–45. But William Holman Hunt brought a painter's prejudices to his work for the medium. Years later he recalled "the disappointment I felt when at first I saw my designs in Moxon's volume. A certain wirelike character in all the lines was to me, as to all artists with like experience, eminently disenchanting" (from Hunt's introduction to *Some Poems by Alfred, Lord Tennyson* [London: Freemantle, 1901], p. xxiii).

Tenniel himself has left no comment on the Dalziels' work, but he did acknowledge that the sight of his *Punch* cartoons, engraved by the shop of Joseph Swain, caused him a "weekly pang." According to Spielmann, pp. 464, 468, Tenniel's extremely hard, light-grey pencil resulted in woodblock drawings that were simply too delicate for Swain to capture in black and white.

18. Rossetti, *Letters*, 1:239.

19. J. R. Harvey, *Victorian Novelists and Their Illustrators* (New York: New York University Press, 1971), pp. 34–43, 199–210; Steig, *Dickens and Phiz*, p. 7; Cohen, *Charles Dickens and His Original Illustrators*, pp. 15–50. Sybille Pantazzi outlines the nineteenth-century tradition of authors "writing up to" preexistent illustrations in "Author and Illustrator: Images in Confrontation," *Victorian Periodicals Newsletter* 9 (1976): 38–49, esp. 39–41. On page 40 she gives the quotation noticed here, from *Finden's Tableaux . . . of National Character*, ed. Mary Russell Mitford (1838). Life also discusses the tradition (which he believes was minor and atypical) in " 'Poetic Naturalism,' " pp. 56–58.

20. De Maré, *Victorian Woodblock Illustrators*, pp. 57–58, 64, 133–34. Reid wryly notices how Thornbury glossed over this practice; see *Illustrators of the Eighteen Sixties*, p. 17. According to Life, " 'Poetic Naturalism,' " p. 58, there were "numerous volumes, mostly issued in the seventies, wedding new texts to illustrations reprinted from books and periodicals." The practice suggests decline, and indeed the era of "the sixties" was coming to an end.

21. Thomas Moore, *Lalla Rookh: An Oriental Romance* (London: Longman, Green & Co., 1861), p. 117; an illustration for the versified story "The Veiled Prophet of Khorassan." Walter Thornbury, *Historical and Legendary Ballads and Songs* (London: Chatto and Windus, 1876), p. 120; for the poem "A Tartar Foray." It is true that Thornbury's melodramatic Persian exoticism is a lot like Moore's.

Figure 11.6 made one other noteworthy appearance in 1861, shortly after it appeared in *Lalla Rookh*. Henry G. Bohn added "a new chapter on the artists of the present day" to the second edition of John Jackson and W. A. Chatto's *A Treatise on Wood Engraving*, which he published that year. Characterizing Tenniel as "a successful illustrator of Historical subjects, and Ballad poetry," as well as a popular contributor to *Punch*, he exemplified the artist's work with three illustrations, of which fig. 11.6 was the most prominently displayed (pp. 559–60). Bohn implies (p. 549) that the various artists chose their own pictures. The *Times* reviewer of *Lalla Rookh* commented favorably on this same picture ("the denouement in the death of Zelica . . . has the element of pathos as well as grace"); and years later Monkhouse displayed it prominently in his monograph on Tenniel, which he prepared with Tenniel's cooperation.

22. J. Hillis Miller, "The Fiction of Realism: *Sketches by Boz, Oliver Twist*, and Cruikshank's Illustrations," *Charles Dickens and George Cruikshank*, ed. Ada B. Nisbet (Los Angeles: William Andrews Clark Memorial Library, 1971), pp. 43–53.

23. *OED*. Although the word *illustrate* acquired its pictorial and its text-related senses by the seventeenth century, the corresponding senses of *illustration* are not on record until the early nineteenth century.

24. Miller, "The Fiction of Realism," p. 45–46.

25. Richard Kelly, " 'If you don't know what a Gryphon is': Text and Illustration in *Alice's Adventures in Wonderland*," *Lewis Carroll: A Celebration—Essays on the Occasion of the 150th Anniversary of Charles Lutwidge Dodgson*, ed. Edward Guiliano (New York: Clarkson N. Potter, 1982), pp. 62–74. John Davis was simply wrong in asserting that "The various characters are meticulously described by Carroll[,] who left little scope for the artist to do much more than embellish the story"; "Introduction" to *The Illustrators of* Alice in Wonderland *and* Through the Looking Glass, ed. Graham Ovenden (London: Academy Editions, 1972), p. 14. Davis tried to explain the similarity between Tenniel's work and the work of later illustrators by supposing that they were all commonly determined by descriptions in Carroll's text.

In 1887, in a review that he wrote of the stage production of *Alice in Wonderland*, Carroll revealed how he "pictured" some of his characters; but in fact his account includes hardly any visual detail, the emphasis being mainly psychological (" 'Alice' on the Stage," *The Lewis Carroll Picture Book*, ed. Stuart Dodgson Collingwood [1899; rpt. Detroit: Tower, 1971], pp. 163–74).

26. Hodnett, *Image and Text*, pp. 6–10.

27. *Alice's Adventures in Wonderland*, illustrated by Barry Moser (Berkeley: University of California Press, 1982). Moser justifies this innovation by complaining that all previous illustrators "have intruded on the privacy of Alice's adventure, standing apart and observing Alice in her dream. They have been voyeurs, and yet there can be no voyeurs to dreams. In *The Pennyroyal Alice* [on the other hand] . . . the images of Alice's dream are always seen from Alice's point of view, for after all, the dream *is* Alice's dream" (p. 143). Moser's point is a double one: the view from outside is both impolite and impossible. But by that logic, the whole of Carroll's narration of Alice's dream is an impolite impossibility.

That said, I would recommend Moser's *Alice* illustrations as the most worthy successor to Tenniel's.

28. There have been three important editions of the *Alice* books that feature colored versions of the Tenniel illustrations. *The Nursery "Alice"* (London: Macmillan & Co., 1890), a greatly simplified adaptation of *Alice's Adventures*, includes twenty enlarged and colored adaptations of the original black-and-white illustrations. Edmund Evans, the leading color printer of the day, used as many as eight color blocks per picture (including black) to match the color tones of pictures that Tenniel had specially colored himself. The first printing of this book was rejected by Carroll because the pictures were "far too bright and gaudy, and vulgarise the whole thing." (A facsimile edition of the more delicate second printing was published by Dover in 1966; a similar edition by Mayflower in 1979—both in New York.) The complex history of this project is laid out by Selwyn H. Goodacre in "The Nursery 'Alice': A Bibliographical Essay," *Jabberwocky* 4 (1975): 100–120.

In 1911, three years before Tenniel's death, Macmillan in London published a one-volume edition of both *Alice* books that included sixteen of Tenniel's illustrations, redrawn and colored, as full-page plates. (Macmillan reissued these plates in a portfolio in 1980, and included them in a New Children's Edition published at that time.) It is not known who prepared these illustrations. Unlike the illustrations for *The Nursery "Alice"*, which had black engraved outlines and resemble hand-colored black-and-white engravings, the 1911 illustrations appear to be done in pencil and watercolor. The colors are much heavier than in *The Nursery "Alice"*—murky, even; and the hues are different. The Gryphon, for example, was green and red in 1890 but turned purple, blue, and brown in 1911; Alice's dress changed from yellow to blue-violet.

In 1946 Random House in New York published editions of the *Alice* books with the Tenniel-Dalziel illustrations "colored in the manner of the period by Fritz Kredel." Kredel applied his watercolor tints with a light hand, leaving many areas white; the general effect is unobtrusive and very attractive. When Alice did dream in color, the colors probably looked like that.

29. Figs. 1.7, 1.18, 1.22, 1.31, 1.40, and 7.5; also 11.7 (cited below).

30. For a similar, more elaborate account of such possible differences, see Joseph H. Schwarcz, *Ways of the Illustrator: Visual Communication in Children's Literature* (Chicago: American Library Association, 1982), pp. 16–18, 93–94. Schwarcz discusses also some twentieth-century illustrations to *Alice*, on pp. 97–99.

31. Layard, *Tennyson and His Pre-Raphaelite Illustrators*, p. 40. Compare Meyer Schapiro, *Words and Pictures: On the Literal and the Symbolic in the Illustration of a Text* (The Hague: Mouton, 1973), p. 11: "Sometimes the text itself is not specific enough to determine a picture, even in the barest form. Where the book of Genesis tells that

Cain killed Abel, one can hardly illustrate the story without showing how the murder was done. But no weapon is mentioned in the text and the artists have to invent the means."

32. An anonymous reader for the Ohio State University Press has pointed out another slip of this kind, much easier to miss: in figure 1.6 it should be Tweedledum who has the wooden sword, not Tweedledee.

33. Anne Clark, *The Real Alice: Lewis Carroll's Dream Child* (London: Michael Joseph, 1981), pp. 105–6. See also her *Lewis Carroll: A Biography* (New York: Schocken, 1979), p. 135.

34. Hodnett, *Image and Text*, p. 179. (It is true that when "Alice looked all round the table . . . there was nothing on it but tea"; but an English tea would normally include milk.) Hodnett criticizes a few other illustrations for oversights; pp. 177, 189.

35. Janis Lull, "The Appliances of Art: The Carroll-Tenniel Collaboration in *Through the Looking-Glass*," *Lewis Carroll: A Celebration*, pp. 101–11.

36. Harry Furniss, "Recollections of 'Lewis Carroll,' " *Strand Magazine*, April 1908, pp. 50, 52.

CHAPTER 12

1. From a lost pamphlet by Carroll, "The Profits of Authorship," as quoted by Collingwood, p. 228.

2. Professor Cohen provides a preview of this correspondence in "Lewis Carroll and the House of Macmillan," *Browning Institute Studies* 7 (1979): 31–70.

3. *Alice's Adventures in Wonderland and Through the Looking-Glass and What Alice Found There*, ed. Roger Lancelyn Green, Oxford English Novels (London: Oxford University Press, 1971), p. 71. The layout of this edition is perpetuated in the Oxford Paperbacks edition of 1975, and in the World's Classics edition, published by Oxford in 1982.

4. *The Complete Works of Lewis Carroll* (New York: Modern Library, 1936), p. 87. *Annotated Alice*, p. 108.

5. *Alice's Adventures in Wonderland and Through the Looking Glass* (1962; rpt. Harmondsworth, Eng.: Puffin-Penguin, 1976), p. 108.

6. *Alice's Adventures in Wonderland* (London: Macmillan & Co., 1866), p. 117. This edition, referred to here as the "first edition" or "original edition" of *Alice's Adventures*, is the first edition to be published, but the second to be printed. As was indicated in chapter 10, the first printing, dated 1865, was suppressed because of defects, on Tenniel's advice. The second printing was entirely reset, but the layout of the two printings is essentially the same. The minor differences in layout, which chiefly involve the removal of "widows" at the tops of some pages, are described by Harry Morgan Ayres, "Carroll's Withdrawal of the 1865 *Alice*," *Huntington Library Bulletin*, no. 6 (1934): 153–63. In a recent essay, Selwyn H. Goodacre amplified Ayres' observation that several of the changes "permitted a better placing of the picture" ("The 1865 *Alice*: A New Appraisal and a Revised Census," *Soaring with the Dodo: Essays on Lewis Carroll's Life and Art*, ed. Edward Guiliano and James R. Kincaid [Silver Spring, Md.: Lewis Carroll Society of North America, 1982], pp. 78–79). For citations of other accounts of these early editions see Crutch, pp. 29–36; and chapter 10, note 2, above.

7. Crutch, plate X. See p. 211, no. 13.

8. *Alice's Adventures in Wonderland*, People's Edition (London: Macmillan & Co., 1887), p. 88.

9. *Alice's Adventures in Wonderland*, Sixpenny Series (1898; rpt. London: Macmillan & Co., 1900), p. 72. For some features of the Sixpenny Series edition see Crutch, p. 235. The cited copy appears to be a copy of this edition, though it is part of a specially bound combination of the two *Alice* books and lacks any series designation. The two separate title pages carry the Macmillan imprint, but the foot of the spine is stamped "SAMMELS [sic] / & TAYLOR"; this is the copy briefly described by Flora

V. Livingston, *The Harcourt Amory Collection of Lewis Carroll in the Harvard College Library* (Cambridge: privately printed, 1932), p. 39, where the name is mistakenly given as "Samuel."

10. *Alice in Wonderland*, ed. Donald J. Gray, Norton Critical Editions (New York: Norton, 1971), p. 54. *Alice's Adventures in Wonderland* (New York: Random House, 1946), p. 76.

11. *Through the Looking-Glass, and What Alice Found There* (London: Macmillan & Co., 1872), pp. 66–67.

12. *Alice's Adventures under Ground: Being a Facsimile of the Original Ms. Book Afterwards Developed into "Alice's Adventures in Wonderland"* (London: Macmillan & Co., 1886), p. 6.

13. Warren Weaver, *Alice·in Many Tongues: The Translations of* Alice in Wonderland (Madison: University of Wisconsin Press, 1964), pp. 39–40 (emphasis added). Facsimile editions of the three translations are: *Aventures d'Alice au pays des merveilles*, trans. Henri Bué (1869; rpt. New York: Dover, 1972); *Alice's Abenteuer im Wunderland*, trans. Antonie Zimmermann (1869; rpt. New York: Dover, 1974); and *Le Avventure d'Alice nel Paese delle Meraviglie*, trans. T. Pietrocòla-Rossetti (1872; rpt. New York: Dover, 1978).

14. Crutch, pp. 36, 64–65. I checked the constancy of these editions to the original formats by comparing copies of the 1906 issue of *Alice's Adventures* and of the 1908 issue of *Looking-Glass* to copies of the original editions in the Houghton Library at Harvard University. I also compared to them a personal copy of the combined issue of the two resettings that was published by Macmillan in New York in 1944.

15. A few features that distinguish the setting of 1866 from that of 1865 are reported by Livingston, *Harcourt Amory Collection*, pp. 12–14. See also Ayres, "Carroll's Withdrawal of the 1865 *Alice*."

So far as I know, the 1865 *Alice* (London: Macmillan & Co.) has never been reproduced in a facsimile edition. But a thousand copies of the 1865 setting were outfitted with new title pages and published by D. Appleton and Co., New York, in 1866; these copies constituted the first American edition; and Appleton published a facsimile of *that* edition in 1927. The foreword to this facsimile alludes to the merits of the original layout: "No format was ever better conceived, more consistent with the spirit of the text than the original edition illustrated by Tenniel."

16. *National Union Catalog: 1956–1967*, no. RL DO 58246; the date and publisher are supplied in brackets.

17. Macmillan published these facsimiles in 1984. Alfred A. Knopf also published them, in New York.

Joan Stevens recognizes the integral placement of other Victorian woodblock illustrations, and criticizes the indifference of modern editions, in two helpful essays: "Thackeray's *Vanity Fair*," *Review of English Literature* 6 (1965):19–38; and "'Woodcuts dropped into the Text': The Illustrations in *The Old Curiosity Shop* and *Barnaby Rudge*," *Studies in Bibliography* 20 (1967):113–33.

Bibliography

The following list includes the major secondary sources cited in the text, as well as a few other items of special relevance to Tenniel.

Allen, Philip Loring. "The Sketch-Books of Wonderland." *Bookman* 26 (1908): 648–51. Compares Tenniel's illustrations for *Alice's Adventures* to the new illustrations then being published in new editions on the expiration of Carroll's copyright.

Bond, W. H. "The Publication of *Alice's Adventures in Wonderland*." *Harvard Library Bulletin* 10 (1956): 306–24. A detailed account, with sidelights on Tenniel's role.

The Brothers Dalziel: A Record of Work, 1840–1890. 1901; rpt. London: B. T. Batsford, 1978. Many scattered references to Tenniel.

C., F. "Tenniel's Book-Illustrations." *Notes and Queries*, 12th ser., 4 (1918): 237–38. A lightly annotated list.

Cohen, Morton N., ed. *The Letters of Lewis Carroll*. 2 vols. New York: Oxford University Press, 1979. Several references to Tenniel.

Collingwood, Frances. "The Carroll-Tenniel Partnership." *Books*, November–December 1964, pp. 232–35. Occasioned by the fiftieth anniversary of Tenniel's death; sees Tenniel's illustrations for *Alice's Adventures* as influenced by Carroll's manuscript illustrations. Criticized by P. H. Muir in a letter to the editor: *Books*, January–February 1965, pp. 30–31.

Collingwood, Stuart Dodgson. *The Life and Letters of Lewis Carroll (Rev. C. L. Dodgson)*. New York: Century, 1899. The authorized biography of Carroll; the source of several anecdotes involving Tenniel.

Crutch, Denis. *The Lewis Carroll Handbook*. Folkestone, Kent: Dawson-Archon, 1979. Revision of Williams and Madan's *Handbook* (see below).

Davis, John N. S. "Artists in Wonderland." *Mr. Dodgson: Nine Lewis Carroll Studies*. London: Lewis Carroll Society, 1973. Brief survey of various illustrations to the *Alice* books, ranging from Victorian times to the present. Similar to Davis's introduction to Ovenden (see below).

"Death of Sir John Tenniel." *Times*, 27 February 1914, p. 11. Obituary.

Gardner, Martin, ed. *The Annotated Alice*. New York: Clarkson N. Potter, 1960. Annotations include occasional remarks on the pictures, summarizing opinion about possible sources.

Green, Roger Lancelyn, ed. *The Diaries of Lewis Carroll*. 2 vols. 1954; rpt. Westport, Conn.: Greenwood, 1971. Many references to Tenniel.

Hartley, Harold. "Lewis Carroll and His Artists and Engravers." *The Lewis Carroll Centenary in London, 1932*, ed. Falconer Madan. London: J. & E. Bumpus, 1932. An appreciative essay on the illustrations for Carroll's various books, by a pioneering collector of sixties material.

Hearn, Michael Patrick. "*Alice's* Other Parent: John Tenniel as Lewis Carroll's Illustrator." *American Book Collector* 4 (May–June 1983):11–20. A compact survey of Tenniel's work for the *Alice* books. Illustrations include proofs, now in the British Museum, of several rejected versions of the woodblock illustrations.

Hodnett, Edward. "Tenniel in Wonderland." *Image and Text: Studies in the Illustration of English Literature*. London: Scolar Press, 1982. A compendious account of the circumstances and merits of the *Alice* illustrations.

Kelly, Richard. " 'If you don't know what a Gryphon is': Text and Illustration in *Alice's Adventures in Wonderland*." *Lewis Carroll: A Celebration—Essays on the Occasion of the 150th Anniversary of Charles Lutwidge Dodgson*, ed. Edward Guiliano. New York: Clarkson N. Potter, 1982. Tenniel's illustrations make up for the lack of visual description in the text of *Alice's Adventures*.

Knight, Jacqueline. "The Theatre of John Tenniel." *Theatre Arts Monthly* 12 (1928): 111–18. Describes and reproduces early theatrical sketches by Tenniel, now in the Harvard College Library.

Lennon, Florence Becker. *Victoria through the Looking-Glass: The Life of Lewis Carroll*. New York: Simon and Schuster, 1945. Includes many references to Tenniel.

Lucy, Henry William. "Sir John Tenniel." *Dictionary of National Biography . . . 1912–1921*, ed. H. W. C. Davis and J. R. H. Weaver. London: Oxford University Press, 1927. Biographical sketch.

Lull, Janis. "The Appliances of Art: The Carroll-Tenniel Collaboration in *Through the Looking-Glass*." *Lewis Carroll: A Celebration—Essays on the Occasion of the 150th Anniversary of Charles Lutwidge Dodgson*, ed. Edward Guiliano. New York: Clarkson N. Potter, 1982. Pays special attention to the synoptic imagery of the frontispiece to *Through the Looking-Glass*.

McGillis, Roderick F. "Tenniel's Turned Rabbit: A Reading of *Alice* with Tenniel's Help." *English Studies in Canada* 3 (1977): 326–35. In general Tenniel emphasizes Alice's desire to be an adult; details of the garden-scene illustration suggest the sexual aspect of this desire.

Mespoulet, Marguerite. *Creators of Wonderland*. New York: Arrow Editions, 1934. Marshals evidence to suggest that both Carroll's text and Tenniel's pictures for the *Alice* books were strongly influenced by the satiric drawings of J. J. Grandville.

Meyer, Susan E. *A Treasury of the Great Children's Book Illustrators*. New York: Abrams, 1983. A chapter on Tenniel reviews the record of his collaboration with Carroll.

Monkhouse, Cosmo. *The Life and Work of Sir John Tenniel, R. I.* London: Art Journal, 1901. A special issue of the *Art Journal*. Mainly biographical, with information supplied by Tenniel himself. Many illustrations.

Morris, Frankie. "Alice and King Chess," *Jabberwocky* 12 (1983): 75–90. Suggests that pantomime costumes influenced Tenniel's Duchess and chessmen.

Ovenden, Graham, ed. *The Illustrators of* Alice in Wonderland *and* Through the Looking Glass. Introduction by John Davis. London: Academy Editions, 1972. 2d ed., 1979. Reproduces dozens of illustrations for *Alice* by various artists, mostly post-Victorian. Includes a list of the many illustrated English-language editions. See Davis (above).

Robb, Brian. "Tenniel's Illustrations to the 'Alice' Books." *Listener* 74 (1965): 310–11. Appreciative essay.

Sarzano, Frances. *Sir John Tenniel.* English Masters of Black-and-White. London: Art and Technics, 1948. Dozens of Tenniel illustrations, from books and magazines, with a compendious introduction. Includes a list of books and magazines illustrated by Tenniel.

Schiller, Justin G. Review of *Tenniel's Alice* (see below). *Jabberwocky* 9 (1980): 104–7. Differs with the editors regarding the classification of the Tenniel drawings at Harvard, and regarding the practices that Tenniel followed in preparing the *Alice* illustrations.

Schwartz, Narda Lacey. "The Dodo and the Caucus Race." *Jabberwocky* 6 (1977): 3–15. Possible sources for Carroll's and Tenniel's drawings of the Dodo. Amplified by a letter to the editor from Brian Sibley, p. 58.

"Sir John Tenniel." *Punch* supplement, 4 March 1914, pp. 1–16. Obituary memoir, with many illustrations from *Punch*.

Spielmann, M. H. "Sir John Tenniel." *Magazine of Art* 18 (1895): 201–7. Informative essay, mainly biographical, based in part on an interview. Largely reprinted in Spielmann's *History of "Punch."*

———. *The History of "Punch."* London: Cassell, 1895. Extensive and detailed, with much information on Tenniel.

Tenniel's Alice: Drawings by Sir John Tenniel for "Alice's Adventures in Wonderland" and "Through the Looking-Glass." Introduction by Eleanor M. Garvey and W. H. Bond. Cambridge: Harvard College Library, 1978. Over two dozen preliminary and finished pencil drawings, reproduced full-size, with an introduction discussing Tenniel's procedures.

Visages d'Alice, ou les illustrations d'Alice. Paris: Gallimard, 1983. A collection of essays and illustrations, supplementing an exhibition; includes some preliminary drawings by Carroll.

Williams, Sidney Herbert, and Falconer Madan. *A Handbook of the Literature of the Rev. C. L. Dodgson (Lewis Carroll).* London: Oxford University Press, 1931. Includes speculations about possible prototypes for the Tenniel illustrations.

Name Index

Subject Index